ONE BREATH

ONE MOVEMENT

HOW TO: EMBRACE CHANGE & EMBODY PEACE THROUGH YOGA

Dan Edelston

This book is for informational purposes only. It is not intended to serve as a substitute for professional medical advice. The author and publisher specifically disclaim any and all liability arising directly or indirectly from the use of any information contained in this book. A health care professional should be consulted regarding your specific medical situation. Any product mentioned in this book does not imply endorsement of that product by the author or publisher.

ISBN- 978-0-9982883-9-0

Disclaimer…

If you're a fan of only positive "woo-woo, new aged nonsense books," you might want to close the cover and look elsewhere.

This book is not about spiritual bypassing. You know telling yourself everything's okay when it's really not, or thinking you've healed all of your issues because you're only thinking positive thoughts.

However, if you're a person who seeks the truth, craves authenticity, and is truly ready to do the work to live a more peaceful and relaxed life, look no further.

As Psychologist Carl Jung said, "One does not become Enlighted by imagining figures of light, but by making the darkness conscious."

If you're ready to make a real, lasting change, you've come to the right place.

Enjoy YOUR journey.

DAN EDELSTON

IV

CONTENTS

Part 4: Taking Action

INTRODUCTION

"The only impossible journey is the one you never begin"

–Tony Robbins

Do you feel your life can sometimes be overwhelming?

Do feelings of fear arise when something in your life unexpectedly changes?

Do you find yourself not living the peaceful life your soul craves?

Within this book, you will learn the exact formula you need to better embrace change and embody peace in your life.

You might find the formula to be simple, but simple doesn't always mean easy.

The information about to enter your brain and being, is a combination of ancient tradition and modern-day physicality.

Not only will you intellectualize the concepts, but you will also begin to FEEL then.

When applied, they can have life-changing benefits.

Before we get into the information, it's important to tell you of why so many people fail at these simple concepts. To become aware of how much struggle there is in people's internal worlds, and what you can do not fall into this trap.

One thing you must understand is that many if not most people are afraid of the dark, specially their own darkness. This isn't to say there are monsters hiding under these people's beds, but they are afraid of , is what Carl Jung called their Shadow Side. This aspect of your personality is your darkness and is something you try to ignore, suppress or repress every day.

If you look carefully enough, you'll see it every day. It can take many forms, but typically it manifests as self-defeating behaviors or that unwillingness to step outside your comfort zone.

It could take form in someone not raising their hand at work in a meeting when they know they should. It could be a person who stays in a job that is absolutely soul-sucking or even an avoidance to introduce themselves to somebody new because of fear or embarrassment.

Many people would rather die, than break outside of their comfort zone. They feel it's scary, unknown, and this can cause a tremendous amount of anxiety.

Simply put, your darkness is an unwillingness to embrace change.

However, as you will learn, change is the only constant in life, it's something you need to learn how to navigate.

This book was created to share the life-changing system that will not only show you how to embrace change and embody peace but shift how you operate in this physical world.

By applying the techniques you'll learn later in this book, you will discover how harmonizing your mind-body connection will open your eyes or even your (eye) to something you never knew.

Through embodying the simple principles, you will put into motion a new way of thinking, a new way of taking action, and a new way of being. You'll soon find yourself inspired to take action while others are fearful! Your mind will change from thinking, "Oh no, what is this change? To "How Can I best navigate this variation in plans"

The system is grounded in 3 ancient practices:

***Yoga**
***Meditation**
***Surrendering**

The majority of this book will focus on yoga, particularly you'll discover the power of using one breath-one movement. You will learn about the history of yoga, how to use the technique and how it has helped so many people embrace change.

Having a better understanding of yoga just might inspire you to join your local studio where you can put the technique into practice. You'll have the urge to have the rubber meet the road, because it's one thing to read about it, it's another thing to take action and feel into it.

Now, the simple practice of yoga could be all you need to transform yourself into that person who takes action, embraces change and becomes more present.

However, for many the embodiment of peace comes when they learn to meditate and practice the art of surrendering. These topics will be addressed and explored toward the end of your reading journey. By the end, you'll have a better understanding of what these topics are, how to apply them and how to objectively see if they are making a difference along your journey.

IMPORTANT...

The tools in this book will only work if you are willing to take action and also explore your dark side.

As you begin to practice, yoga, meditate and learn to let go; a number of negative thoughts, feelings and emotions will come to the surface.

There will be times where you doubt yourself, want to quit, think it's nonsense or even question the meaning of your life.

When these feelings arise, don't quit, use them as an opportunity to acknowledge your resistance and keep going deeper.

This is simply your ego trying to keep you in place, to stay safe and not to grow.

Does this barrier to growth sounds like it could prevent you from embracing change?

Right now could you think of examples where you've started to make a change for the better and then something stopped you, held you back or even sabotaged you?

It could have been a lack of motivation, the negativity of a friend or family member or possibly your own negative self-worth.

This is a common issue many of us face, and it especially manifests in yoga.

As a yoga teacher, I see students chose classes that are "easier" and slower-paced. Typically, they report taking these classes because they feel accomplished, that they can keep up and they know what they are doing.

Unfortunately, their practice not only stagnates in the physical realm but their mental, emotional and spiritual growth also seems to remain the same as they are not being challenged.

As American writer, William S. Borroughs says, *"When you stop growing, you start dying". "In this world you are either growing or you're dying, so get in motion and grow."* [1]

How does this manifest in yoga?

The inability to breath in various postures, the frustrations when having to hold a balancing posture for a period of time and constant movement in the meditative part of class known as Savasana when there isn't music.

It can also show up with frustrated huffs and puffs when a teacher does try to incorporate a challenging, pose, sequence or change to the typical class. Instead of embracing the change, students "half ass" their way through whatever the teacher is providing, never being fully present.

It may sound obvious, but If you're never brought to your edge, how can you grow? How can you become the person you were destined to become?

The only difference between a diamond and a lump of coal is pressure!

Now, this doesn't mean you have to stress, hustle or grind your way through this process. It's actually quite the opposite. It's about finding a balance of effort and ease when moving throughout your day.

It's about how accomplishing your goals and living life can come from your heart and not your ego. Instead of wasting your time, trying to fill a void, you'll find that your heart is full and you do things out of passion. You'll want to share your gifts and kindness with others to make the world a better place.

This all might sound too good to be true. You might think that is hippy-dippy bullshit!

Or maybe you're thinking, "I'm supposed to embrace my dark side, but also live from my heart."

How can this be?

It's quite a paradox indeed!

As you attempt to reconcile it, realize you cannot have the light without darkness, you can't embrace change if things weren't changing and you can't have peace if there wasn't any conflict.

Rather than constantly being at the mercy of life's extremes, and feeling polarized, you'll find more calmness and sense of being centered. Operating from this state of being will allow you to open your heart and take action from the beautiful space.

Interestingly enough, many people would share the same frustrations as you when it comes to understand these paradoxes. However, as they begin to practice yoga, meditate and surrender, something changes.

Something inside you will begin to shift. You might think you've been living life all wrong, or why didn't I find this sooner?

You'll even learn about celebrities who felt the same way, but have discovered the life-changing difference yoga has made in their lives. While we should never worship high-status people or put them on a pedestal, we can simply acknowledge that success does leave clues.

Self-Reflection

At the end of every chapter, you will come across "An Invitation to Explore."

These sections were created to allow you to tap into your feelings about what you just learned. Too often in life, we might read something interesting, watch a video on YouTube or hear about a topic on a podcast. Instead of reflecting on how we feel about it, we immediately intellectualize it. We let our Egoic mind think about every angle of the subject and overanalyze it. While there is value in intellectual thought, conversations, and discussions, too often than not, we are constantly thinking about something rather than observing how our soul and heart feel about it.

This prevents us from truly embodying a concept.

As you close out each chapter, you'll be asked to "explore, meditate, reflect or journal" on how the topic made you feel.

It's an invitation, not a requirement. However, to get the most out of this book it is highly encouraged!

There is so much beneficial information ahead of you that I can't wait for you to get started.

Before you take that step, there is one more thing.

Many people think of yoga teachers as Guru's, even put these people on a pedestal like a celebrity. If you've watched the Netflix documentary, "Bikhram: Yogi, Guru, Predator", you saw the devastating consequences of how some people elevated to this status can cause serious harm.

Throughout this book, I attempt in every way to not make it about me or profess the I'm some enlightened being.

To be honest, I'm just a guy who has been fortunate enough to teach others the beauty of yoga. This lucky and phenomenal opportunity opened the door for me to give a TEDx Talk about the power of Yoga.

As you read on, don't think of it like Dan as having all the answers. Instead, this book is about the proven techniques that so many people before me have successfully used to transform their lives.

I simply collected the information, applied it to myself and students as well as learned how to organize it.
Simply put, consider me the messenger, a bridge between information of what you don't know and what you don't even know you didn't know.

At the end of the day, you are the master, you are the captain of your own ship, and deep down inside you, you know you have all the answers. You simply just need a guide to bring you to your own door of self-discovery.

I am grateful you have chosen me to be one of your many guides on your journey.

Namaste,

Dan Edelston

Part 1: THE PROBLEM

XVIII

CHAPTER 1

YOU NEED TO EMBRACE CHANGE

"I have accepted fear as a part of life. Specifically the fear of change. I have gone ahead despite the pounding in the heart that says: turn back"

– *Erica Jong*

As you begin this journey of self-exploration, give yourself permission to say:

"Life can sometimes be challenging."

Now ask yourself, how does it feel to be authentic and admit this truth?

Because throughout your days, you are faced with many challenges and changes. Sometimes it's the challenge of having to be around toxic people at family gatherings, work, or other social situations.

You know that person who is always negative and loves to complain about the latest event they heard on the news, what somebody did to them or how they were mistreated. They love to tell you every detail of the story and talk incessantly about how the world is unfair. They end up draining any positive energy you did have before that conversation. You leave feeling exhausted, tired, and in a bad mood. You might immediately picture someone in your life who jumps right into your mind.

Maybe you're experiencing trouble with your finances. At your core, you crave financial freedom, having enough money to be truly free and spend every minute of the day how you want too.

Unless you've acquired such wealth, you might be stressed when it comes to paying the bills, feeling frustrated that you have to live on a budget, or even work a second job just to make ends meet. If you're in a relationship, there might be many challenging moments of agreeing upon what to buy and how to budget. One of you might want to spend while the other wants to save.

How about the challenge of living with yourself? Those times in life that you fail at something you wanted to achieve. When this happens to do notice that you are you unfairly judging yourself? Being overly critical? Saying things to yourself in your own head that you would never dare to say out loud? Does your inner world mimic a peaceful beach on a beautiful sunny day, or is a Category 5 hurricane barreling down on the coast?

A whole book could be written just on your life's challenges up until this point. Let's be real, you've been through a lot. Some things you've overcome; other things you are still holding onto. A part of you deep down knows there will be more challenges to come.

You might even avoid any challenging situations by living in your comfort zone. You know, play it safe, do just enough to get by, only do things you're familiar with. Your ego tries to control everything leaving you feeling lost and searching for meaning. But if you live like this, deep down, you feel stuck, and your soul craves new stimulation as well as connections.

Life Is Always Changing

As the saying from ancient Greece goes, "The only constant in life is change."[2]

Sometimes it's the day to day changes like the weather, your: emotions, thoughts, and attitudes. Other times there are more life-altering events such as: being fired from a job, having a romantic relationship come to an end, or even losing a loved one. Whatever the change might be, one thing is for sure. It can be difficult to embrace change.

Intellectually you know change is happening, but emotionally you struggle to accept it.

This change can create a feeling of doubt, insecurity, and fear about our future.

Much of your suffering has to do with the challenge of change, specifically how you might have moments of failing to embrace change.

When you don't embrace change, many issues arise.

Anxiety is a common problem amongst many Americans, if not for people all over the world. When something is about to change or has changed, we experience anxiety about what the future holds. We worry what will be the next step, how will we move forward, how will this change my life?

Take, for example, a relationship coming to an end. Many of us had experienced going from the highest high of being in love to the lowest low of that relationship coming to an end. You feel the pain of losing love, that powerful force that made you feel alive, connected, and whole.

You feel like a shell of yourself, unsure of what to do.

Do you try to re-build the relationship that was lost? Do you decide to go on as many dates as possible in an attempt to move on? Do you take time to be alone and sit with all of your feelings? It can feel like there is no right answer, and everything you attempt to do, does not make the situation improve.

Then the anxiety of what to do next continues to build: What do you do around the holidays? Can you still be friends with their friends? What if you go out and see your ex with someone else having a great time?

Anxiety could even manifest in day to day changes. Some of us getting anxious when we had our whole day planned, and then something changes. A meeting might have been pushed back, but you can't make it because you have to pick up your kids or have other obligations during that time. Maybe you thought you were going to have dinner with just one friend, and then they ended up bringing someone else that changes the whole social dynamic. Or maybe you woke up late and you're full of anxiety about whether you'll get to work on time, hope your boss doesn't know and complete all of your required tasks.

Throughout your studies and internet searches, you may have heard that anxiety is considered, "worrying about the future." If that's true, then depression is all about harping on the past.

Take, for instance, your romantic relationship that ended. Instead of concerns about how to move forward, you instead, dwell on what you had. You think about the vacations you went on, the restaurants where you dined, or even the plans you had for the future. The change was so dramatic and painful, you're having a difficult time coming to process it and let go. You might even have feelings of anger or apathy mixed in as well.

The same gloomy feelings can happen in your day-to-day. That lunch you planned with your best friend for weeks, was canceled at the last second and now you're feeling sad. The weather app told you it was going to be a beautiful sunny day, then you went outside and it started to rain, making you somewhat upset that your day is now ruined. Even in your conversations, somebody was negative, said something that wasn't nice, and now you feel bad about yourself. It was only a minor comment, but now you're hearing it on and endless loop in your head.

What changed?

You were feeling good, and now you're unsure of yourself and feeling down.

Anxiety and depression are two common symptoms of not embracing change. Many, if not all, of us will experience these feelings when the time comes for something new in our lives.

However, if we don't actively work on how we navigate change, we might develop phobias.

A phobia is a fear of a particular stimulus.

One such phobia about change is "Metathesiophobia."

A person who is "diagnosed" with this condition has been categorized as having a "reduced will to live." Essentially, they turn down any opportunity or situation that might involve change. People with this condition feel they have no control over their lives. To adapt, they become rigid in their own routines and refuse to step outside their comfort zone.[3]

When they do confront change, they experience full-blown anxiety and panic attacks.

To avoid having those episodes, a person will go to great

lengths to avoid pain. They will tell lies, make excuses, and even cut off family and social ties.

Many people are aware of their condition but feel they are unable to overcome it.

Now you might be reading all of this and think, "This is pretty heavy and negative stuff."

Or, "Wow, there are a lot of problems and suffering from not embracing change."

Whatever you are thinking and feeling in this present moment, that is okay. Do not judge yourself. Being authentic with your feelings is one of the first steps to learning the power of embracing change.

The goal here is not to persuade you to feel anyway. Instead, it is only bringing awareness to what happens when you don't embrace change.

The more you pay attention, the more you will see this issue in your interactions with family, friends, and coworkers. If you really listen and connect with the person you are talking too, you will begin to notice where they are not embracing change. You'll see what kind of pain it causes them. You'll see in precisely what areas of their lives they stay in their comfort zones.

More Than Mental & Emotional Suffering

As we just discussed, the issue of not embracing change can manifest on the mental and emotional side with depression, anxiety, and phobias.

However, this same problem can also manifest in your physical body.

When you don't embrace change, you become stressed, and stress has numerous side effects on the body.

Western Science has conducted research and is now verifying how stress can affect us on a physical level.

For instance, WebMD.com states physical symptoms of stress include:

"Low energy, headaches, upset stomach, aches, pains, tight muscles, chest pain, insomnia, frequent colds, loss of sexual desire, dry mouth, nervousness, and many more." [4]

The bodily experience of an emotion is felt nearly instantaneously. Within the first few seconds of experiencing something negative or stressful, you automatically tense your muscles. Typically, this takes place in the jaw, stomach, or shoulders.

Think about it, even if someone makes you flinch, what do you do with your body?

When your body is stressed, your muscles become tense, which decreases blood flow, leading to lower oxygen delivery and the accumulation of toxic metabolites. Additionally, your muscles are shortened, which can activate pain receptors. [5]

The validity and empirically proven results of science clearly demonstrate the problems we can experience from not embracing change.

But what do the ancient teachings of yoga and eastern medicine say about the effect of stress on our bodies?

Many yoga teachers and those in eastern medicine believe you tend to store your emotional stress in your physical hips. Objectively, more research needs to be conducted. However, almost anyone who performs a naturalistic observation or takes a yoga class can attest to emotions being stored in their body.

In the yogic world, there is a pose called "Half Pigeon" This stretch is designed to get deep into your hip to stretch the muscles, tendons, and ligaments. Somewhere in between the 3 to 5-minute mark of being in this pose, something happens. It doesn't occur in every class, or for every person, but this is the pose where you can see some people visibly sobbing. The pose allows people to let go, especially if they have been storing their emotions and not finding a way to express them. Be sure to google this connection on your own, or maybe take a yoga class to experience it for yourself.

A recent study did find a connection between the jaw and the hips. It was discovered that when a person worked on releasing and relaxing their jaw, the range of motion of their hips significantly increased. [6] This finding indicates that there is so much to the mind-body connection, which we still don't understand.

Another area of the physical body that responds to emotional and mental stress is the Psoas Muscle. This muscle runs from the 12th thoracic vertebrae and into the pelvis and femur. Its primary function is to stabilize our lower back and assist with hip rotation and walking. [7]

Due to stress, this muscle can become tight. When you experience a stressful situation, you tend to hunch over and draw your belly inward. It's a survival mechanism that is built into us.

Picture yourself when you were a child. Was there something you can remember that scared you and made you curl up into a ball? Or maybe as you got older, someone went to punch you or jumped out at you to scare you and can you drew everything in for protection.

Eastern medicine believes these negative emotions are stored in our Psoas. When you have a tight Psoas, you will most likely also experience back pain.

In a yoga class, when poses are used that assist in stretching the Psoas, there have also been first-hand accounts of people releasing emotions when that muscle is elongated. They might be in a pose as simple as lying on their back and drawing one knee in to their chest, but you can see tears running down their cheeks. Any person with a curious mind would think there has to be something to this!

Later on, we will share an exercise specific to releasing emotions in your body so you can experience the release for yourself.

Much of the work we do in yoga comes from FEELING. Our intellectual mind can only take us so far.

But for now, all you have to understand is that there are numerous consequences to not embracing change. There are signs on the physical, mental, and emotional levels. Having any unresolved negative issue in your being will hold you back from living your best life. They will make you feel less than you are and cause you to feel something is wrong with you.

If you feel you are experiencing any of these symptoms, fear not.

As mentioned earlier, we are merely trying to authentically acknowledge and accept what is going on. If we don't know the territory, we can't begin to explore it.

This book was written with solutions on how to embrace change and live a more peaceful life. Just like anything in life, it is a journey. Be sure to enjoy each step as you make your way through this book.

An Invitation To Explore

Now that you know about the physical, mental, and emotional manifestations of not embracing change. We wanted to extend an open invitation for you to explore your mental, emotional, physical problems of not embracing change.

Take time to truly tune into how you might be experiences negative conditions on these various levels.

Do you have physical symptoms? where are they?

Do you have mental unrest? How does it manifest?

Do you feel negativity? How so?

I'd invite you to explore, meditate, reflect, or journal on how not embracing change could affect you on a spiritual level.

Feel free to share the information with others or acknowledge it as your own sacred knowledge.

Bonus Invitation

The information you have learned thus far, has not truly addressed your spiritual level of being.

Spirituality can mean so many things to so many different people. For some, it is merely their connection to the various individuals in their lives. For others, it is their connection with the universe. Some people say they are spiritual and not religious, and they just want to treat people with respect and love. And for some spirituality could explore Wicca, Meditation, Yoga, mystery schools, or esoteric knowledge.

Whatever spirituality is for you, I'd invite you to explore, meditate, reflect, or journal on how not embracing change could affect you on a spiritual level.

You might find this aspect of you has not been connected with in quite some time.

CHAPTER 2

MISSED OPPORTUNITIES

"Don't Fear Change, Embrace It."

- Anthony J. Dangelo

Since the beginning of time, millions upon millions of people who have failed to embrace change.

Whether it was out of fear, anxiety or stubbornness, this inability to accept change has had devastating consequences.

The failure to embrace life's variations manifests in numerous ways: Missed opportunities to learn, make connections, build friendships, improve health, keep up to speed with technology, and maybe the most painful of all, lost financial opportunities.

When looking at our fellow humans on this planet, we can't s see the internal thoughts and emotions of what they are going through. However, their physical being, their external tends to be used as a benchmark to measure how this person is doing. We can see it with our eyes and use it as a tangible evidence to understand what might be going on in the inside. For instance, a person walking around with their head down might indicate that they have low self-esteem. Somebody who constantly taps their foot or shakes their leg back and forth demonstrates feelings of being anxious. An individual who is constantly looking around the room while you're speaking shows an overactive mind that can't focus.

These are simple examples of how body language suggests what's going on with the internal mind of an individual.

Even more profound examples can be seen with the internal mindset of cooperation's. Specifically, those individuals in charge of making big decisions.

Take, for example, the now out business company known as Blockbuster. You might be too young to remember, but some of us can remember driving to a physical store to rent a movie that came in a blue and white plastic box. When the film wasn't sold out, we stand in line, pay to rent it, and then make the drive back home to watch it.

Days later, we'd go back to the same store just to return it. If you are old enough to remember taking home a VHS tape, you would have to rewind it or otherwise be charged a fee. If you didn't return a move on time, you'd also be charged another fee which could quickly add up, especially if life became busy and you forgot to bring it back.

In the year 2000, just as the world was changing with the convenience of the internet, a small startup company named Netflix approached Blockbuster offering to sell a stake in their company.

The meeting was months in the making. Netflix reached out insensately over many months to meet with Blockbuster. Then one day, the executives at Netflix were told to be in Dallas, Texas, the next day at 11:30 AM. At the time, Netflix executives were over 12 hours away. Desperate, the co-founders of the company spent $20,000 to charter a private plane to make the meeting. As it turns out, it was the Vanna White's jet. Yes, the Vanna White from Wheel of Fortune.

Netflix executives were able to make it to Dallas, and during meeting Co-Founder, Reed Hastings said;

"We should join forces," he said. "We will run the online part of the combined business. You will focus on the stores. We will find the synergies that come from the combination, and it will truly be a case of the whole being greater than the sum of its parts." [8]

Blockbuster executives asked Netflix who much they wanted for this opportunity.

When CEO of Netflix said, 50 million dollars, it was reported John Antico, the CEO of Blockbuster, was trying not to laugh at the offer.

Mr. Antico thought Netflix was a niche business and turned down the proposal.

It's unfortunate he failed to embrace the changing technology of the time because…

As of the year 2019, Netflix is worth close to a trillion dollars, and Blockbuster has only one niche store in the world!

Cell Phones Too

Another attention-grabbing example of the failure to embrace change involves the cell phone company Blackberry. In the early 2000s, the business was valued around 83 million dollars.

Initially, the Blackberry was the phone of the businessman. In 2003 the company released its 7230 device, which was considered the smartphone and could be used to answer e-mails and navigate the internet. The phone had a tactile, pushbutton keyboard built right onto the device. It was like having a mini computer in your pocket.

Celebrates soon began using the phone, as well. Well- known names like Kim Kardashian and Paris Hiltons were spotted using these devices in magazines and on television. Soon, consumers wanted these same very phones that they saw wealthy businessmen and celebrities using.

If you had a Blackberry between 2003-2007, you were considered to be "cool." You'd show it off to your friends and they were amazed by what this form of technology could do.

You had the power to send a text message almost immediately, while others had to use their flip phones. It would take them forever to respond because they would have to the number seven, (4) times in a row, just to use the letter S.

Around 2007, Blackberry heard that competitor Apple was releasing its I Phone. This device as your probably well aware allowed users to use a digital keyboard. The digital interface came up only when you needed to type a message, browse the web, or send an e-mail on your phone. This created more screen space and gave users a new and unique experience.

Instead of Blackberry embracing this fantastic technology and putting all his resources to immediately compete, CEO Mike Lazaridis said in 2008 after the I-Phone was already launched,

"The most exciting mobile trend is... Full Qwerty keyboards. I'm sorry, it really is. I'm not making this up. People are running out of their two-year contracts, and they're coming into the stores, and they want to be able to do Facebook, and they want to be able to do instant messaging, and they want to be able to do e-mail and they ask for those features thinking that they're going to get another flip phone and they're walking out with a (BlackBerry) Curve or a Pearl because they're the best devices for doing those kinds of activities. And so, what is the defining factor? The keyboard." [9]

Blackberry took over a year and a half before finally releasing their Blackberry Storm to compete with Apple. Unfortunately, it was difficult to use, sluggish, and their mobile web browser could not efficiently handle complex web pages.

On June 16th, 2008, Blackberry's market capitalization or total market share price was 81.66 billion dollars.

Around the same time in June 2008, Apple released its second I phone, the I phone 3G. Apple was able to fix many issues from its initial phone. As a result, the stock value of Blackberry dropped all the way down to 21.66 billion dollars. That is a drop of over $60 Billion, yes Billion dollars in half a year!

As of October 21st, 2019, Blackberry's total value is 2.88 billion dollars. On that very same day Apple, reported market capitalization of over 1 trillion dollars! [10]

Today, Blackberry is almost a forgotten and irrelevant company on the consumer level, especially compared to Apple.

Speaking of Apple, Ronald Wayne was a lesser-known individual who co-founded the company with Steve Jobs and Steve Wozniak in 1976. Wayne wrote Apple's computer manual. He also designed their initial logo, which was an image of Sir Isaac Newton, the man who created the law of gravity sitting underneath an Apple tree.

Wayne was a 10% minority owner but was given the rights to tie-breaking decisions between the two Steve's.

During this time, he was in his early 40's and was reported to be opposed to taking risks. Years earlier, he had lost money and gone bankrupt on a slot machine business.

Afraid to take what he considered a risk and not embrace change, he decided Apple was not for him. After just 12 days of being with the company, he decided to bail and take his $800 investment with him.

Wayne believed, "he was standing in the shadows of giants" when it came to product design talent. [11]

He was also quoted to say he knew Apple “"would be successful, but at the same time there would be significant bumps along the way, and I couldn't risk it.

Today, his net worth is estimated to be around $400,000. If he had kept his 10% share, he would have close to 95 billion dollars. [12]

Have you ever turned down a new opportunity due to your age? Have you ever had a gut feeling that something was going to work out but decided to stay in your comfort zone anyway?

As you can see by these cooperate examples, there are significant consequences to not embracing change. The world is always changing, and when you've had success doing something and making money off of it, it can be difficult to all of a sudden switch gears and change how you do things. While it might be easy to criticize these individuals, we can all take solace in remembering that at some point, we have missed out on financial opportunities by staying in our comfort zones.

In addition to missed opportunities in the finical business world, there are many other examples of missed opportunities in our culture.

Burt Reynolds, who started acting in 1958, had played numerous roles on television and in movies. You may know him for his mustache or from some of his films such as "Boogie Nights or "Strip Tease." He had a long-lasting career, and at some point, you've probably heard his name. However, for many of us we, "kind of know about him."

If I say the name Burt Reynolds what is the first thing that comes to your mind?
In Burt's career there were multiple opportunities he missed out on to become an even more memorable actor. Instead of remembering him as the guy with the mustache, you could have known him as having some of the most iconic roles of all time.

In 1965, Burt had the opportunity to play the famous role of James Bond after Sean Connery decided to walk away from the part. The bond role or 007 is a character who works as a British Spy. He lives a life of intrigue as he solves a crime, has relationships with beautiful women, and exudes a cool, calm, and collective demeanor.

It's the role of a lifetime for many, and when Burt was asked to play James Bond, he turned it down because he believed that the public wouldn't accept an American 007.

Burt turned down the idea of the movie studio changing from traditional British actors and allowing an American to play the role.

Of course, other non-British actors went on to play James Bond, such as Peirce Bronson, George Lazenby, and Barry Nelson.

Imagine how many things in your life you said no to because of what you thought someone else would think of you or if they would accept you?

Later in 2015, Burt was quoted,

“It was a stupid thing to say, I could have done it, and I could have done it well.” [13]

Unfortunately for Burt, he did not learn his lesson of embracing change.

In 1975, a man named George Lucas was looking for actors to play characters in his science fiction movie called "Star Wars."

There was a character named Han Solo, and the writers felt Burt would be perfect for it.

Even if you are not a Star Wars fan, you at some point have most likely heard of the movie in conversation or on social media.

When offered the role, Reynolds turned it down. (Palm smacking face emoji)

In an interview with Business Insider in 2016, he said, "He regretted turning it down."

"I just didn't want to play that kind of role at the time." [14]

Instead of embracing the change to play a new kind of character, Burt would instead act in other movies, such as "Gator," "Semi-Tough," as well as "Smokey and the Bandit." Movies many of us have never heard of.

Have you had an experience where someone asked you to do something that was outside of your comfort zone or not what you're used too? And you turned down there offer and later regretted it?

Whether you have a beautiful big mustache or not, we've all pulled a Burt Reynolds at some point in our lives.

One More Example

Not only do we encounter the pain of not embracing change in cooperation's and amongst celebrities, but we also see it in our history.
Historical examples are phenomenal ways for us to learn from our past.

"Those who fail to learn from history are doomed to repeat it."
- George Santyana [15]

Take for instance the United States of America.

The revolutionary war, the fight for an independent country from Great Britain, started on April 19th, 1775. There are many reasons as to why this war started. But unfair taxation, especially with the Stamp Act, created a revolt, and tea was thrown into the Boston Harbor.

As rebellions formed, a war with the British became inevitable. The Americans, many who were farmers, were not trained in military tactics. The British, wearing red coats, had years of experience, and knew how to fight in battle. Desperate, the Americans led a guerilla warfare style attack against the British under the guidance of General George Washington.

Later in 1775, American forces had suffered multiple defeats. British General, William Howe had the ideal opportunity to end the rebellion with a battle at Valley Forge.

By nature, Howe was a conservative, competent technician. Instead of being aggressive, CHANGING his strategy, and going on the attack, he decided to hold off. [16]

As we know, the Americans would later win the war, and the 13 colonies would become the United States of America.
He resigned in 1778 amongst pressure from the British government to step down. Howe would later write his memoires that he recognized his failure.

As you can see, there are many examples of people who have not embraced changed. For some, this cost them billions of dollars, others a more profound legacy, and for another being able to change the course of history entirely.

If you live in the United States, and if General Howe had embraced change, life would be much different.

Could you imagine? We might only have Tea at our local Starbucks. Soccer, and Rugby would be the national sports, and we'd say "Ello Governor" to each other! Well, maybe not that last one, but it would sure be different.

An Invitation To Explore

These historical examples serve to create knowledgeable and tangible evidence of what can happen when you don't embrace change. They also serve as an example of what happens when you don't take a step of your comfort zone.

We wanted to extend an open invitation for you to explore in what areas of have you not embraced change? Is there an area of your life where you look back and find a sense of regret? Thoughts like "if only" or even just the idea of how your life might look different today?
This exercise isn't too make you feel bad, to get upset or feel regret. Instead, if there is anything we can learn from history, it is that if we don't learn lessons, it is doomed to repeat itself.

You might already have some ideas in your head that pop right up. What if you had taken that job? Asked that person out? Or speak up for yourself during a challenging time?

I'd invite you to explore, meditate, reflect, or journal on where you feel you did not embrace change.

Try not to label, judge, or see these events as unfavorable. They happened, and depending on the circumstance, there might not be anything you can do. And that's okay.

What's important is the recognition and the hope and understanding that the future you will learn the tools in this book of how to recognize, sense, and step forward into the positive changes you will improve your life.

CHAPTER 3

A PERONAL EXAMPLE

"Being on a spiritual path does not prevent you from facing times of darkness, but it teaches you how to use the darkness as a tool to grow."

- *Unknown.*

As you continue on this journey, I wanted to let you know that this chapter details what I personally went through with learning the pain of not embracing change.

When writing this book, I did not want to make it about me. My intention is to provide YOU with useful information on what exactly YOU can to embrace change and live a more peaceful life.

As you know, we live in a society that is heavily influenced by social media, where people share all the positive things going on in their lives. Depending on your interpretation, you might consider these posts to be nothing more than people bragging, or you might see the images as inspiration.

Whatever your viewpoint, I want you to know through my purest intention that the following only serves to let you know where the idea of this book came from and to only be used as inspiration.

Now that we have that out of the way, let's go back to April 4th, 2016. I'm sure this day is probably just a blur in your mind, but for me, it's a day I'll never forget.

On that evening, I was lying in bed, starting up at the ceiling fan of my bedroom, slowly spinning around. I couldn't sleep, not only because I knew how dusty the fan was, but I was distraught, devastated, and demoralized over a heart-wrenching breakup. The woman who I thought I was going to marry and spend my life with was no longer my significant other.

Have you ever found yourself in a relationship that started out absolutely amazing? You were incredibly attracted to this person; you shared the same interests, finished each other's sentences, and looked forward to getting home from work to spend time with the love of your life?

This was the person I was engaged too, and I was looking forward to our future. In fact, we had all the details planned out of where we were going to live, the type of house we would buy, even small details like the color of a couch or the style of furniture was discussed and planned. We also considered retiring to a coastal town in Maine to live close to the ocean and eat delicious lobster.

Like any relationship, it can be a challenge to maintain the initial spark, that lust, the unbridled passion you have toward that person. At first, you might ignore little quirks or even red flags because of the feeling you have been with this person. However, as time goes on and the initial newness wears off, you begin to see things differently.

The things you used to find to be adorable now annoy you. Why do they always play the music so loud while they are getting ready? Why doesn't she leave me alone when I'm in a bad mood? Why does she always want me to watch these boring shows with her?

On top of that, communication begins to change. Instead of keeping an open line of conversations, life gets busier, more obligations come your way, and you find yourself not talking and flirting like you used too. Everything becomes an organizational question: what time are we leaving? Did you pick up the wine for the party? Why are you wearing that? There isn't an emotional connection; instead, it turns into ego, intellectual chatter.

At some point, there then comes a moment in a relationship when trust is tested. And when that trust is broken, resentment builds.

This is what happened to me. I'm sure you can think back to someone you dated, where your trust was tested.

And to be authentic and honest with you, it was my fault. There was no cheating, no flirting with other women, but there were little white lies.

Lies that were created in my mind to protect her and not hurt her. For instance, one time, we were out enjoying a delicious dinner, when I ran into a woman I used to date.

Now, objectively, many people would say this woman was just as beautiful and intelligent as my fiancée. She waved hello and gave me a big smile as she walked by, I looked up and said, "Hi." That was it…

My fiancée immediately grilled me with multiple questions, "Who's that?" "How do you know her?" Did you sleep with her? "I could sense she felt somewhat threated by this woman and the interaction. Feeling the pressure of wanting to keep the happiness of our relationship and not to upset my fiancé in any way, I lied. I told her that she goes to my gym and that nothing had happened between us. Instead of speaking my truth, I became a coward and lied.

Of course, every lie in life eventually comes to the surface. Weeks later, through a little social media digging and knowing a friend of a friend, she found out that I did in-fact date this woman. She was furious, and that's where the resentment began.

Have you ever lied to someone or caught someone lying? What did it do to your relationship? Many people have said, lying is just as wrong as cheating because the foundation of which your partnership is built takes a tremendous hit. It's almost like a gigantic earthquake in California rumbling the grounds of your tiny home.

Once she found out, any other thing I lied about, no matter how small, destroyed her trust in me. Eventually, we came to a crossroads where she decided it was no longer going to work out. The woman of my dreams, the person who I was going to build something beautiful with, was gone.

The days afterward, I found myself lacking an appetite, the motivation to do anything productive, and the inability to sleep.

Have you ever had a relationship come to an end, and you realize that you've lost a complete sense of who you are as a person? That this individual provided you with that sense of feeling whole? That the relationship itself gave purpose and meaning to life?

In those days, that's how I felt, living a life where I needed all the external validation to feel whole on the inside.

Fast forward to a week later, and there I am, lying in my bed, starting up at that dusty ceiling fan.

I was in a dark place. But then I remembered I had been in dark places before. Seeing my dad leave me at a young age, being bullied in school, witnessing the severity of family alcoholism, and so much more. We all experience darkness, but when we do, we can use it to suffer or as a tool to grow.

As I lay there, I had all of those images come to mind and realized, I am still here, I survived all of these tough times, and I can make it through where I am right now.

At that moment, I told myself to let it go. That there is some higher power out there. Call it the universe, God, or whatever you believe in, there is something out there bigger to ourselves.

As I truly let go, that's when I heard a voice come into my head. It's difficult to explain, it wasn't like I was clearly hearing a voice like a person who is a medium or someone with schizophrenia. It was this feeling, a knowing, and my mind read it out loud, just as you are reading these words in your own head.

The voice said,

"You're feeling overwhelmed, Breath, You're feeling stuck, "Move."

The answer came through so; clearly, it felt like Morgan Freeman was narrating the solution.

Breathe and move, it sounded so simple.

Sometimes in life, the answers to our problems are felt in our hearts, rather than through our intellect.

I kept thinking, where could I go to learn this? Is there a book? A video? A course?

And then I let that thinking go.

A few moments later, I saw an image of myself doing yoga.

Yoga was there answer!

I googled my local studio and decided to try Vinyasa Flow.

On the class description, it even said: "Learn how to go with the Flow."

The message was obvious. I was living in my head, overthinking everything, and doing the exact opposite of going with the flow.

My First Yoga Class

As I walked into my first yoga class, I immediately felt insecure. There was one muscular guy with his shirt off doing handstands, a woman in a forward fold with her head on her thighs and some other woman doing some sort of crazy arm balance. Everyone was in tremendous shape, happy, and had yoga clothes on. I was nervous, a little chubby, and was wearing basketball shorts with a "shmedium" shirt.

The instructor told us to find a seated position before the start of class. She began chanting, lighting incense, and talking about energy. What the heck did I get myself into?

As the class progressed, she had us do these weird things called Sun Salutations. She taught us something called a Chaturunga, which involved learning how to move your body into an upward facing dog and then into a downward-facing dog.

All I could think about was how strange this experience was and that I was completely outside my comfort zone. As we moved throughout the class, I felt like the tinman, I couldn't get myself into the positions other students were moving into so effortlessly.

Near the end of the class, we began to lie on our backs for something called Savasana. I love naps, so I laid down and closed my eyes....

And then something strange happened. A clear liquid began rolling down the side of my face. I was crying! What the heck was going on?

As the class came to an end and we said "Namaste," I asked the instructor if this was normal. She told me people tend to release all sorts of things here on the mental, emotional, and physical levels. She encouraged me to continue with the practice.

I decided to commit to yoga 5 days per week. Mainly because I noticed how everyone in the class seemed so relaxed, happy, and were in incredible shape.

Within a month, I was able to learn how to control my breathing and put myself through many challenging poses. What was once difficult became a lot more manageable. In fact, I was enjoying myself. There was a significant sense of accomplishment of being able to do something I wasn't previously able to do.

I was feeling happier, more relaxed, and optimistic about my future.

This motivation then transferred off my mat. Simple things like changing the residential address on my bank account, throwing away old photos of my relationship, finding a new place to live, or working though each emotion became easier.

Within a few days, I was no longer staring at my ceiling fan, and within 30 days, I felt the change.

I started to think to myself, what is happening? what is it about yoga that is changing my life for the better?

As I was driving one day, I realized that instead of always being in my head, paralyzed by what to do next, over analyzing every little detail of my life, I was taking everything one breath one movement at a time.
If something gave me anxiety or depression, I would take a breath and think of what action I could choose to move forward with my life. This enabled me to slow everything down and is the core essence of what you will learn about in this book.

As the days passed, I continued to go to yoga, and pretty soon, people began to notice the change in me. They asked what I was doing, "are you taking medication? Are you on drugs? Are you losing your mind?

When I told them yoga, they laughed and said it was woo-woo hippy, new-age nonsense.

However, I encouraged them to come to a class with me, and told them if they didn't like it, I'd buy them dinner.

After dealing with much resistance and endless jokes, they finally agreed to come.

Guess what happened? They came, and they loved it!!

I'm happy they did because, at the time, finances were extremely tight. My fancy dinner for them would include the dollar menu at McDonalds.

Inspired by my own change and those of others, I enrolled in a yoga teacher training program.

That experience taught me how I could share the gift of yoga with others.

Before long, I found myself in front of class teaching others. As new students arrived, I noticed they were full of physical and mental restlessness. They would fall out of poses, forget to breathe, and always move around in the meditative part of a class known as Savasana.

During these moments, you could see the frustration in people's minds and bodies. You could see how they were judging themselves and beating themselves up for not getting in the poses. After class, they would discuss how they are not flexible and how yoga is not for them.

As those students came up to me, I simply encouraged them to keep to practice each week. Those that did had profound transformations you could physically see.

They began to hold their ground in balancing poses, linking breath with movement, and lie still in Savasana. They reported feeling "good," "in the flow," "relaxed."

The point of discussing this journey isn't too brag. In fact, a yoga teacher is just a vessel during the class. The student is the master, the master of how their bodies move, the emotions that come up, and their mental mindset. A teacher is simply there just to lead them to a door, it is up to them to open it.

With this story, I hope you are beginning to see the power of yoga. Specifically, how taking everything one breath, one movement at a time, can transform your life and give you peace of mind.

If you have ever thought you're not flexible enough for yoga, fear not.

In a later chapter, we will discuss, what yoga is, and how we are all exceptional at it!

In the meantime, let's take some time to explore your thoughts and feelings.

An Invitation To Explore

Now that you are aware of the power of one breath and one movement.

We wanted to extend an open invitation for you to explore precisely what areas of your life you feel overwhelmed in.

Think of the various domains of your existence. Your physical health, finances, relationships, spirituality, emotions, thoughts, behaviors, routines, or even your habits.

I'd invite you to explore, meditate, reflect, or journal on where you feel overwhelmed.

Whatever you find, try not to judge or label anything. Simply acknowledge it because later on, we will discuss how to break it down into simple action steps, to give you peace of mind.

Part 2: THE SOLUTION

CHAPTER 4

WHAT IS YOGA?

"Yoga is the journey of the self, through the self, to the self."

- *The Bhagavad Gita.*

If you were to ask the next ten people you saw, what yoga is? You would mostly likely get ten different answers.

Some might tell you that yoga is life-changing, others might explain how they wouldn't; be caught dead in a yoga class, while others might say they've heard it's great for stretching.

Is yoga walking into your local boutique studio to exercise in a hot and sweaty ninety-five-degree environment? Is it traveling to India to meet with a guru who has a beard that is longer than the red carpet at the Academy Awards? Is it turning yourself into a pretzel?

Technically, this is all yoga, but the real answer goes beyond any stereotypical version you may have heard of. In its most straightforward modern-day western definition yoga means, "to yoke, to bind, to bring together." Or the particular version I was reminded about, "One Breath-One Movement."

To really understand what this practice is all about, we must go back in time.

We must travel back to the beginning, and start with the Yoga Sutras.

The Yoga Sutras are a collection of 196 different teachings which date back over 4000 years on the theory and practice of yoga. It is believed an Indian Sage by the name of Patanjali put together this work. There are questions as to whether he wrote all of the sutras, but regardless he is known for creating the earliest inception of yoga.

From the 12th to 19th century the works were nearly forgotten until a now famous Hindu Monk named Swami Vivekananda began introduced these works to the people of India.

According to the first sutra 1.2, "Yoga is the inhibition of the modifications of the mind. Vivekananda translates the sutra as "Restraining the mind-stuff." [17]

Primarily, yoga was created for us to have better control over our minds. The sutras give us 8 limbs to follow to obtain this calm mind and reach a step closer toward enlightenment.

The eight limbs include: Yama (abstinences), niyama (observances), asana (yoga postures), pranayama (breath control), pratyahara (withdrawal of the senses), Dharana (concentration), Dhyana (meditation) and samadhi (absorption) [18]

1. Yamas:

Yamas are about how we can learn to abstain from negative influences. As we know, to live a purer life, we need to stay away from things that can hold us back, such as drugs, alcohol, sleep deprivation, eating unhealthy foods, and so much more.

According to Yoga Sutra 2.30, there are five Yamas we should adhere to as ethical rules or moral imperatives. These include 1. Ahisma: non-violence, not harming other beings. 2. Satya: to be true, non- falsehood. 3. Asteya : not to steal. 4. Brahmacharya : chastity, marital fidelity, and sexual restraint. 5. Aparigraha : non-avarice, non-possessiveness. [19]

It is believed all of these restraints help in the self-development and growth of an individual.

Can you think of an area in your life where you might need more self-restraints? Is there anywhere you are sabotaging yourself by not abstaining from negative influences?

Some Yogi's feel that Yama's are similar to the ten commandments of Christianity. It's almost the rules of what not to do to live with less suffering.

2. Niyamas

Niyamas, the second limb and are all about virtuous habits, behaviors, and observances.

If the Yamas told us what not to do, the Niyamas tell us how we should live our lives.

First is, Shaucha: purity, clearness of mind, body, and speech. Second, Santosha is the acceptance of others, acceptance of one's circumstance, contentment. Third Tapas are persistence, perseverance, austerity. Fourth, Svadhyaya is the study of self, self-reflection, introspection of thoughts, speeches, and actions. Fifth, Ishvaarapranidhana is contemplation of the true self. [20]

It is interesting how the sutras start off by telling us what not to do. Some yogi's claim it's organized that way because we must make space, clear away and create boundaries for the things we can later do.

You might be thinking I have to do all of this to do yoga?... "This sounds exhausting!"

Don't worry… you do not have to adhere to everything in the sutras to "do yoga." Everything you are learning is just to understand the history of yoga and to take ONLY WHAT YOU NEED to live your best life.

Some people spend their whole lives studying the sutras in an attempt to embody the principles, while others just go to a yoga class. There is no right or wrong way to "do yoga"

As you continue reading, you'll understand how One Breath and One Movement is the ideal starting point for your yogic journey.

Speaking of movement...

3. Asana

Asanas are the postures. If you look at any Sanskrit name for most yoga postures, you'll hear, Trikonasana, Gomukhasana, or even Savasana. These postures are where we get the movement in our yogic practice.

However, according to the Sutras, Asana is only a meditation posture that a person holds where they are steady and motionless. It was believed there were 12 different seated postures a person could assume to sit for meditation.

But wait, I thought you said Asanas are movements?

Technically in the early teachings of yoga they are not

However, as we finish the sutras, you will soon learn how movement was created as yoga continued to change with the changing times.

4. Pranayama

Pranayama is comprised of two words Prana which means breath and Ayama to expand, stretch, and restrain.

According to the Sutras, after a pose (asana) was established, a yogi then engaged in the practice of consciously regulating their breath. There were many different breathing techniques created. A popular one you may have heard of his "Ujayi" this Sanskrit words means to be victorious. I like to think of it as a victorious breath over your thoughts, emotions, and feelings.

This breath is used in many Vinyasa yogic practices, and for many, is established as linking one breath to one movement.

5. Pratyahara

Pratyahara comprised of two words, Prati, meaning contra, and ahara, meaning bring near.

Essentially, this term means to stop being controlled by the outside world. Instead, we begin to seek knowledge and understanding of our inner world.

The first four limbs of yoga focused on the outside world. Pratyahara is a bridge to shifting our awareness to our inner world. It enables us not to be phased by external stimuli.

Image what your life would be if you were able to not react to everything that came your way? Finding calmness in situations where many people would overreact?

This limb of yoga has helped me significantly in my "road rage." For many years I would beep my horn, give a finger, or flash my lights at other drivers who weren't adhering to my egoic standards of how people should drive. But then, through embodying this sutra and with time, I was able to become non-reactive. Instead of me yelling at my windshield, my car has turned into a sanctuary where I can find peace.

Can you think of an area in your life where you immediately respond to an external situation in a negative manner?

This sutra shifts you from reacting to everything into a state of responding to anything that comes your way. You go from being out of control, to having control.

6. Dharana

Dharana means concentration and focus.

It's about holding your mind to a singular concentration. Many people use mantras or place their awareness on one particular part of their body. The ability to focus builds one's willpower and ability not to let their mind drift and wander during meditation.

In a world full of constant stimuli such as scrolling through social media and watching television with bright colors, our senses are constantly being bombarded. All of this energy thrown in our face makes us scared, unable to focus, and leaves us constantly bouncing from one thing to the next. It shortens our attention span, such as if a YouTube video isn't less than 60 seconds, we won't watch it, or if an online article requires a scroll or two; we won't even read it.

Now, more than ever, the ability to focus is an asset in today's society. Learning to embody this limb of yoga can create dramatic changes in your life.

Can you think of areas in your life where you need more focus? What comes to mind is how to live more by this sutra?

7. Dhyana

Dhyana means contemplation and reflection.

Ideally, it is the non-judgmental observation of an object. If Dharana means to focus, Dhyana is when you become engaged with that focus. You begin to see layers to what you are focusing on without giving it any labels. Translation, you are the observer.

Throughout this book, I have asked you questions. Every time a question is asked, the intent is for you to embody Dhayana. Not to judge yourself, but to simply observe all of the aspects and forms that come from your own personal answer.

8. Samadhi

Samadhi means putting together, joining, and creating union. Essentially oneness with the subject of meditation.

Translators of this limb believe, "Samadhi is that spiritual state when one's mind is so absorbed in whatever it is contemplating on, that the mind loses the sense of its own identity. The thinker, the thought process, and the thought fuse with the subject of thought."

This limb is challenging to intellectualize; it is something that needs to be experienced. The closest I can personally come to describing it is.... That state of flow you receive when your caught up in a moment OR that feeling after a delighted cry when everything just seems at peace. It's the one limb of yoga that for many find difficult to achieve.

Interestingly, the last limb of the Sutras, Samadhi, means to create union just as the western definition of yoga means to form a union.

The Sutra's in Your Life

The 8 limbs of yoga are something that, when studied, worked upon and embraced can have significant positive changes in your life.

As you were reading them, how did you feel? Did it feel like something that brought you comfort and a knowing that would lead to a better life?

Or did you read through them and think, "They are interesting, but I'm really here just to learn about techniques I can apply right now such as One Breath, One Movement.

Whether you study the sutras or embrace the modern-day definition of yoga, one this for sure...

Whatever version of yoga you decide to open yourself up to, you'll discover an opportunity to embrace change and embody peace more easily.

Post-Classical Yoga

Centuries after Patanjali wrote the sutras, yoga masters began to branch away from tradition. Yogis wanted to bring more life, vitality, and overall energy to the body. It was believed that the path to enlightenment lies in the physical body. Out of this idea, Tantra Yoga was created.

Now you might be thinking, Tantra? Isn't that what the singer, Sting uses to have sex for hours on end?

Technically, Tantra Yoga might improve your sex life because it helps you get more in touch with the subtle energies of your body.

If you're curious you might take the time to Google this topic. If you do, you'll learn more about this practice, specifically about its intricacies. But be cautious, I can't promise you all of the images and articles that pop-up will be Safe for Work, so Googler beware!

Primarily, this practice was established to "cleanse the mind and body. As well as break up the knots to our physical existence. Tantra yoga believes that our body is the key to enlightenment. [21]

Tantra means to weave or expand. It combines the mental and emotional components of the sutras and uses the body for exploration. The sutras involved very little use of the body, where Tantra brought the body to the forefront.

Tantra yoga led to what many of us know as Hatha Yoga.

Hatha Yoga

Hatha means union through the discipline of force. This was the first style of yoga that stressed mastery of the body as the key to enlightenment.

It is believed it made its first debut in the west when Swami Vivekananda provided a lecture at the Parliament of Legions in Chicago, Illinois in 1893. [22]

For those of you curious, the event was a World's Fair in honor of Christopher Columbus's 400-year anniversary of discovery America.

Year later, in 1924, a yoga teacher named, T. Krishnamachary opened the first yoga school in Mysore India. Because of this, some call him the Father of Modern Yoga. He would later mentor three students B.K.S. Iyengar, T.K.V. Desikachar, and Pattabhi Jois. Iyengar and Jois created the primary forms of yoga in the U.S. today.

Iyengar yoga is based out of Hatha yoga. The main focus in this style of yoga is all about your alignment. If you attend an Iyengar type of class,, you will hold poses for some time enabling you to get deeper into the pose. Or as many yogis feel, allowing the pose to get into your body.

B.K.S. Iyengar believed if we can achieve balance in the body, we can calm our minds. Many believe this type of yoga is ideal for people with injuries, beginners, or if a student wants to learn more about alignment. Typically, props are used in this practice to deepen stretches and hold poses for more extended periods. Many Iyengar studios even have ropes attached to the walls as a central focus of their training.

The Iyengar model of yoga is very interesting and quite practical. You might even try a few classes to better understand what the practice is all about.

While practical, this book is grounded in the foundation and fidelity of a modern version of Pattabhi Jois's style of yoga.

Jois created what is known as Ashtanga Yoga. The style of yoga went on to evolve into what in the West call we Vinyasa Flow yoga.

In these practices ujjayi breath is used to link break and movement. This type of breathing focuses on breathing in and out through your nose with a victorious life force breath. This style of yoga is designed to calm your mind while simultaneously cleansing the inner body. Jois believed your muscle strength increases through various repetitions of postures and that your lung capacity also improves. During the practice, you increase your heart rate, as you sweat, which Jois beleived to purify your body. [23]

The method also consists of Sun Salutations before going into what's called standing series poses, which include triangle, extended side angle, wide-legged forward folds, and more.

As Joi's yoga grew in popularity in morphed in Ashtanga Vinyasa and later Vinyasa.

Vinyasa added on more other elements.

For instance, if you attend a Vinyasa yoga class, you might experience the following.

- A seated, lying down, childs pose, or some position that allows you to close your eyes and check into your practice
- A slow-moving warmup, typically on the ground to begin to bring movement into your body
- Sun Salutation A to warm up your spine
- Sun Salutation B to warm up your hips
- Sun Salutation C to work your whole body
- Static holding poses or balancing poses
- Yin, or restorative poses
- Savasana.

Every yoga studio can vary in their approach to Vinyasa, but this is a typical structure you'll find.

Why Should I Know All Of This?

All of the information presented to you is for your general understanding of what modern day yoga is all about.

There isn't a particular style of Western yoga that is "true yoga." Yoga practiced in the west today has veered far off from the initial writings in the sutras.

Some people may attend a Vinyasa class and say, "that's not yoga," or they might go to other styles such as Iyengar and say, "that's not yoga." Technically it's all yoga."

The beauty of Vinyasa classes are you use one breath and one movement to navigate through poses. It does not give you time to think, because you have to keep moving. You build heat from within, challenge yourself, and find a release at the end. It trains your brain that when there is constant change, stress, and a lot going on, you can remain calm and take everything coming your way one breath one movement at a time both on and off your mat.

An Invitation To Explore

Now that you are more aware of the history of yoga.

We wanted to extend an open invitation for you to explore your perceptions of yoga.

Have they changed? Did you already know this information or did your whole perspective on the practice change?

I used too always to think yoga was just a weird thing hippies and guys with man buns would do. But when I learned about the history of it, I realized it was the original model of self-development for growth to embrace change and an understanding of how to live a more peaceful life.

I'd invite you to explore, meditate, reflect, or journal on what yoga now means to you.

CHAPTER 5

THE SCIENCE OF YOGA

Science knows no country, because knowledge belongs to humanity, and is the torch which illuminates the world."-

-Louis Pasteur

Sometimes learning about the history of yoga and hearing how other people have benefited from the practice might be enough to get you onto your mat.

While for others, you might want to know what you are getting yourself into.

Questions such as: What exactly is this practice going to do for me? How does it work? Is this whole thing a placebo effect? Are people convincing themselves about how great it is, when it's really not working?

If you find yourself on the skeptical side or just want to know the science of yoga, this is your opportunity to tumble down the rabbit hole. Over the last 10 to 15 years, extensive research has been conducted and is proving just how about beneficial yoga can be.

Stress

Wherever you live on this spinning ball hurling through space we call earth, at some point in your day, you are going to encounter stress.

Because of this stress, you might have heard people say to live a stress-free life, have no stress, or limit your stress. While this idea, in theory, sounds lovely a practical application and understanding is that we need to have some "good stress" in our lives.

For instance, a person with osteoporosis can benefit from the stress of lifting weights to strengthen their bones. When we stress a muscle, it grows back stronger. If our core muscles are engaged by stress, such as being in a high plank position, they become stronger. When we hold any pose in a yoga class for a long time, we put healthy stress onto our bodies and later enjoy the release of coming out of the pose. Despite new-age attempts to eliminate stress, you do need some stress in our lives to become stronger.

However, stress can become unhealthy when we encounter what is known as "negative stress." This form of tension can manifest in many ways. For instance, the emotional and mental stress of living in faced pace Western culture can cause you to always be on edge, feeling antsy. Having to do all of the things on your to-do list, sitting in traffic, rushing around to get to a place on time, all while trying to make it home it time for dinner is not the most peaceful way to live. On top of all of these expectations you feel you have to adhere too, the overall blueprint of our society has become somewhat sedentary. We leave our house to sit in a car and drive to work only to sit at work and then drive back home to sit on the couch. Not only is this causing weight gain, but the lack of movement is not giving us an outlet to release our stress.

When you are stressed out with "bad stress", your body releases a chemical called cortisol. Cortisol is mostly thought of as the hormone released from the adrenal glands during a fight or flight response. When you have high levels of this hormone surging throughout your body, you might experience: headaches, anxiety, depression, trouble sleeping, problems with digestion, and even weight gain.[24]

A lot of that "muffin top" you may have seen on yourself or another person can be the result of high cortisol levels.

Thankfully there is a solution… and you guess it… yoga!

Yoga can help lower the levels of this stress hormone.

But how?

The Science of Yoga

Throughout the course of a a Vinyassa Flow yoga class, you are warming your body up and performing many different movements. Your body then decreases levels of what's called "monoamine oxidase," or MO, an enzyme released from your liver. As MO levels become lower, so to do your cortisol levels (CITE). [25]

Another empirical study, found after 8 weeks of continuous Vinyasa yoga practice for 3 days per week, cortisol levels amongst yogis were significantly lower than the control group.

According to the results,

"Plasma cortisol was significantly decreased in the yoga group after 8-week yoga training, compared with the CONTROL Group" [26]

If you're feeling stress, or have any of the symptoms of stress, you might want to head to your local studio to experience the practice.

Anxiety

When you experience stress in your life, a natural result of that stimulus is anxiety. However, not all anxiety can be labeled "bad." Some anxiety can manifest as excitement, such as: the feeling before going on a first date, an interview for a new job, moving into a new home or really any feeling you have as you're waiting for something in the future that hasn't happened yet. Sometimes you can easily mistake and label excitement as anxiety.

Conversely, anxiety can also show up in unfavorable ways such as: feelings of danger and panic, rapid heartbeat, rapid breathing, stomach issues, not being able to focus and feeling incredibly overwhelmed to the point that you cancel necessary appointments, avoid people or don't leave your house to avoid stress that could cause anxiety. This form of anxiety is considered "a condition" as it can significantly interfere with the quality your life and daily living.

Every year, millions of Americans turn to their doctors for a pill to relieve their symptoms. While the medication can work, there are issues when people stop taking the drug or experience many side effects while using it.

Feel free to google the side effects of anti-anxiety medications. You'll find there are four classifications: Selective serotonin reuptake inhibitor (SSRI), Serotonin-norepinephrine reuptake inhibitors, Tricyclic antidepressants, and Benzodiazepines.

Each group has their own side effects which can vary from dizziness, fatigue, weight gain, sleep problems, sexual dysfunction and much more.

***Note**, this book is not to give medical advice, if you are on an anti-anxiety medication, always talk to your doctor before you stop taking your prescription. Likewise, if you feel you need to be on an anti-anxiety treatment, speak with your doctor.

Yoga is much different than taking medication. It's something you can do without having many side effects wreaking havoc on your body.

And now research is showing how just how yoga can improve anxiety.

How so you might ask?

Buckle in and throw on your pocket protector, because we're about to get super nerdy.

The Science of Yoga

Yoga leads to an inhibition of the posterior side of your hypothalamus. The main job of the hypothalamus is to regulate emotions and release hormones. Yoga, "optimizes your body's sympathetic or (automatic) response to stressful stimuli and also restores autonomic regulatory reflex mechanisms associated with stress." [27]

Translation, this means yoga inhibits the areas of your brain responsible for fear, aggressiveness, and other emotions. As a a result, it stimulates reward pleasure centers in your brain, causing you to feel more at ease. This allows anxiety levels to decrease, as well as your heart rate, blood pressure, and cardiac output.

If you're feeling anxious or struggle with an anxiety disorder, you might want to head to your local yoga studio to experience the practice. To see just how it feels in your body when the posterior side of your hypothalamus is inhibited.

Depression

If anxiety is a fear of the future, then depression most certainly pertains when you dwell in the past.

One thing that's become clear over the years of practicing yoga is that it is okay to have moments or days when your down, sad, not feeling full of life. If something terrible happened to you, it's okay not to feel full of joy. Being fired from a job, having a romantic relationship come to an end, or even losing a loved one is a good time to allow yourself to feel sad. For some reason instead, we try to not feel and tell ourselves we will be okay. We try to bypass the feelings when sometimes the best thing is to simply acknowledge the emotions in order to begin to heal.

In the western woo-woo new aged world, some believe that you must be happy all the time, to overlook any negative feelings because you're going to attract negativity into your life. While it is true that always being negative will manifest undesirable results you still have to live from authenticity to find joy and come out of depression. In fact, those that are always being fake happy positive, are usually the most depressed people on earth behind closed doors.

Unfortunately, a mindset of only living in the positive, leads to people labeling their feelings of sadness as a bad thing when, in fact they are very normal. So normal, that they are simply a feedback mechanism to assist you in acknowledging something may be off.

Ideally, to heal, we should acknowledge that we feel sad, sit with the feelings, work through them by writing, therapy, solitude or whatever resonates with you. Then eventually come to a place of acceptance and letting go which we will cover later on this book.

The problem arises when depression lasts for prolonged periods, causing severe issues in your daily functioning. That prolonged numbness can take away your joy, your ability to work, or even your ability to heal.

Similar to anxiety, many people turn to pharmaceutical drugs to combat their depression.

The side effects of anti-depressants are similar to anti-anxiety medications. Feel free to refer to the previous section if you wanted to be reminded of what these drugs can do to your body.

*__Note,__ this book is not to give medical advice, if you are on an anti-depressant medication, always talk to your doctor before coming off. Likewise, if you feel you need to be on an anti-depressant medication, speak with your doctor.

Sometimes there can be a tendency to say, "just do yoga" you don't need anti-depressants. While coming from a good place with beautiful intentions, it's just not practical.

In the long-term a person can do yoga and eventually ween off anti-depressants, but it takes time.

Because yoga is not an overnight miracle solution, the recommendations of a medical professional are strongly advised before coming off an anti-depressant medication.

Now that we have that clarified, let's learn how yoga can naturally help to improve feelings of depression.

The Science of Yoga

Yoga increases levels of serotonin levels in your brain. Serotonin is a brain neurotransmitter that is responsible for your feelings of happiness and well-being. Higher levels of serotonin help you feel good, while lower levels make you feel depressed.

Interestingly, 90% of the human body's serotonin is located in your GI tract in your enterochromaffin cells. Something to consider the next time you hear the word gut health…

Back to the science. In addition to increasing serotonin levels yoga also inhibits the posterior side of your hypothalamus, which, as you now know, stimulates the pleasure centers in your brain, allowing you feel more at ease and even blissful. [28]

If you're feeling depressed or struggling with major depression, you might want to head to your local yoga studio to experience the practice, to see just how it feels in your body when the posterior side of your hypothalamus is inhibited.

Overactive Mind

The business of life and endless amounts of social media, especially in the western world, has led to many of us experiencing an overactive mind.

For instance, have you ever had trouble falling asleep because of all of your racing thoughts, or maybe you couldn't focus on one thing because your mind was all over the place?

Some people take pharmaceutical drugs to calm their mind, some take "smart drugs," some drink while others might partake in marijuana.

You could do all of that, or you could try yoga.

The Science of Yoga

During a yogic practice, as you use your breath, you stimulate what's called your Vegas Nerves. These nerves connect from your brain to your body and are responsible for transmitting information. As these nerves are stimulated, a chemical called acetylcholine is released. When acetylcholine enters your bloodstream, it then sends a message to your parasympathetic nervous system.

As this part of your nervous systems is turned on, it produces a calm and relaxed feeling in your body. It takes you out of that fight or flight mode that while responsible for your survival, in high amounts leaves you feeling on edge. [29]

The more you practice yoga, you begin to explore how it feels to have your parasympathetic nervous system activated Some yogis have said that feeling you have at the end of class during Savasana is similar to how it feels after a message or even right after sex.

Blood Pressure

If you have or know of anyone who has high blood pressure, you know it's a severe issue. High blood pressure occurs when there is too much of a force of blood being pumped against your artery walls. While many of us can experience this with stress once in a while, having high levels on a daily basis can cause major problems.

Uncontrolled, high blood pressure can lead to heart attacks, stroke, aneurysms, and even dementia.

Many sedentary people with poor diets and high stress turn to prescription medications to combat high blood pressure.

***Note,** this book is not to give medical advice, if you are on a high blood pressure medication, always talk to your doctor before coming off. Likewise, if you feel you need to be on high blood pressure medications, speak with your doctor.

Symptoms of high blood pressure medication can include: headaches, nausea, vomiting, erection problems, feeling light-headed, diarrhea, constipation, and more.

Yoga, has been empirically proven to improve high blood pressure levels.

The Science of Yoga

Yoga can elevate levels of gamma-aminobutyric A.KA. GABA, a brain neurotransmitter. GABA blocks impulses between nerve cells in your brain. As you move throughout a yogic practice, GABA levels increase, and your blood pressure decreases. [30]

Not Flexible, Poor Balance

Many people get into yoga for the physical benefits. They want to improve their posture, increase range of motion, or become more flexible.

There is no doubt, yoga absolutely works on the physical level.

The Science of Yoga

In a group of college athletes, a 10-week study was conducted to determine the impact of yoga. Three basic assessments were used, a sit and reach test, shoulder flexibility, and a stork stand balance test.

You can think of a sit and reach test as you sit down on the ground, extend your legs and then reach for your toes. A downward facing dog was used to test shoulder flexibility and a Stork Balance test is similar to a tree pose, only with your hands on your hips.

After ten weeks' researchers found the following:

For the sit and reach test, participants who practiced yoga gained an average of 1.5 inches reach of flexibility. Meaning they could extend and extra 1.5 inches, those in the non-yoga control group lost an average of .5 inches, proving that yoga just might help you reach your toes, or at least get your closer.

The shoulder flexibility test found the yogic group had an increase of .5 inches of shoulder flexibility while the non-yoga group lost more than .5 inches of flexibility.

In terms of the balance of the stork stand test, the yoga group improved their overall balance endurance time by an average of 3 seconds while the non-yoga group lost more than 4 overall seconds of holding. [31]

Could Yoga Re-Program Your Mind?

During my TEDx talk, "Embracing Change Through Yoga", I discussed how a yoga mat is your subconscious training ground to re-program your mind.

In a yoga class, you're consciously putting yourself in a challenging situation with constant change of directions and balancing postures. Instead of getting stuck and overwhelmed, you begin to train your brain to take action and navigate this challenging environment, one breath, one movement at a time.

Your mind becomes conditioned that when there is stress, uncertainty, and constant change, you can remain calm and move forward. You embody an action taking behavior both on and off your mat.

Everything else in life feels easier after putting yourself in such a difficult environment. And if something off your mat does stress you out, you can simply take one breath and one movement to navigate whatever environment you're in.

A study in 2019, analyzed the benefits of yoga for 100 prison inmates.

One of the researchers named, Nora Kerekes said,

"One can regulate, for example, impulsive behaviors with different pharmacological interventions, but an increased character maturity suggests personal capacity to handle and overcome both external and internal difficulties, including the control over mental reaction patterns, abilities and drives." [32]

Essentially yoga can assist a person in having control over oneself and the ability to handle external and internal difficulties with more ease.

An Invitation To Explore

Now that you are more aware of the science of yoga.

There is an open invitation for you to explore your intellectual thoughts of yoga.

Have they changed? Did you already know this information or do your whole perspective on the practice change?

For years, you may have heard about yoga, but did you scientifically understand how it was working?

I'd invite you to explore, meditate, reflect, or journal on what the science of yoga now means to you.

CHAPTER 6

CELEBRITY SUCCESS WITH YOGA

"Intelligence is the ability to adapt to change"

-Stephen Hawkins

Earlier in this book, your learned about memorable examples of companies and people who did not embrace change.

Imagine how different the world would look if Blockbuster merged with Netflix? If Blackberry put all of their efforts into touch screen phones and if Ronald Wayne had stayed with Apple? Not only did these individuals miss out on shaping the world, but they lost out on immense financial possibilities.

While some fail to adapt, others learn to embrace it.

The following list of celebrities is presented to you to serve as inspiration of the power of embracing change.

Robert Downey, Jr.

When people hear this name, a few ideas come to mind... former drug addict, years of sobriety, or most likely "Iron Man."

In 1996 the actor was arrested for speeding down Sunset BVLD in Hollywood, California. Upon approaching the car, officers found possession of heroin, cocaine, and .357 Magnum handgun. After his release from jail, he continued to struggle with drug use. He was arrested again in April of 2001, suspected of being under the influence of a stimulant.

After coming out of rehab, the actor would spend the next four years finding work in a few small roles.

However, everything changed in 2008 when he was selected to play the role of "Iron Man" in 2008. Casted as Tony Stark, Downey Jr. made the character a massive success with his witty and dry sarcasm. It was the first of the Marvel movies, created momentum for the franchise to pull in over 22.5 billion dollars throughout 23 films.

To go from a drug addict on the verge of jail time to one of the most popular actors took a significant change for this individual.

An interview from Time Magazine encapsulates the power of yoga in Robert Downey Junior's life.

Here is how that interview with Time Magazine unfolded, (pun intended)

Supine on a love seat in his home at the end of a leafy cul-de-sac in Brentwood, Calif., Downey attempts to explain his improbable comeback. Like many of his stories, this one meanders poetically and involves, oh, several hundred kung-fu metaphors. "I've just been at the ready, and when the opening was there, I hit it," Downey says. "Guard your centerline, watch the lead elbow, look for an opening, make contact, exchange, advance, or retreat and stay connected." **He's fit, mellow and reflective after a morning of power-flow yoga with his teacher Vinnie Marino, part of what could be called Team New Downey, a large coterie that includes yogis, massage therapists, martial-arts instructors and people who know about herbs.** "I need a lot of support... Life is really hard, and I don't see some active benevolent force out there. I see it as basically a really cool survival game. You get on the right side of the tracks, and you now are actually working with what some people would call magic." [33]

Iron Man, I mean Downey Jr, has discovered the power of one breath and one movement during his power flow yoga.

Jennifer Aniston

Jennifer Anniston was known by many as the character Rachel Green on the hit TV show friends. When the show ended in 2004, she was left with a choice. She could either try to find a new television show to star on or branch out, try something new, and change her image. Instead of pigeon holing herself on television, she decided to step into the unknown. Since that decision, she has gone on to play numerous roles in movies such as: "Marlee and Me, Horrible Bosses and We're the Millers". Jennifer is also a spokesperson for Smart Water and Aveeno skincare.

To maintain a thriving career, she's had to embrace change. She has said," "Yoga.... kind of helps you prepare for everything, honestly" "It's like meditation. It sort of just allows anything that's coming at you at the end of the day to be kind of doable."

She's also said, "Yoga calms me down, it gives me energy and focus."[34]

Madonna

The singer Madonna, had her first major hit "Like a Virgin," hit the airways in 1984. Since that the 80's she's continuously embraced changed by re-inventing her look, image, and even her music. Over the years she's built upon her success with 68 Grammy nominations and has released 14 studio albums. As she continued to put out music hit after hit, her style of music has even evolved throughout her career.

How has she learned to embrace change?

Through Ashtanga Yoga!
After the birth of her daughter in 1996, she was looking to get back in shape to maintain her image. It is reported her trainer at the time, Carlos Leon, encouraged her to try Ashtanga Yoga.

Apparently, she really like it because she was so inspired by the practice that on her "Ray of Light" album, she opens with an Ashtanga chant. She even went on to play a yoga teacher in the movie "The Next Best Thing."

This Iconic woman has said,

"Yoga… is a metaphor for life. You have to take it really slowly. You can't rush. You can't skip to the next position. You find yourself in very humiliating situations, but you can't judge yourself. You just have to breathe and let go. It is a workout for your mind, your body, and your soul." [35]

When you have a chance, be sure to google images of Madonna and yoga. She can impressively bend her body into many shapes, which highlights the commitment to her practice.

Tom Brady

Tom Brady, an NFL Quarterback has played 19 seasons in the National Football League (NFL), has won 6 Super Bowls, and is still playing football at the age of 42. To achieve this goal, he has had to continually embrace change to compete at such a high level. He's had to modify his nutrition, sleeping patterns, and even his physical exercise.

Known, as of the most clutch performers in the history of football, he's reported to say,

"Yoga is great for flexibility, it's therapeutic and great for your attitude. And it gets you some silence during your day."[36]

The average career length of an NFL quarterback is three years. Tom has been able to play for more than 6x the average individual.

When selling his Chestnut Hill, Massachusetts home in 2019, the real estate listing reports the residence has its own yoga studio!

Clearly, Tom is committed to his practice.

Brady was also seen performing a High Karate and Airplane yoga pose during an August 29th, 2019 pre-season NFL game vs. the New York Giants!

Reed Hastings

Remember the story of Netflix?

Well the CEO Reed Hastings gave a presentation in 2016 in which he said,

" *Take Care of Yourself" All work and no play isn't the answer, Executives need to take time to develop new skills, cross-fertilize by talking to other executives, and even learn to partake in YOGA.*" [37]

He has also said,

"At my first company, I should have done Yoga. I didn't understand that by making myself better, I was helping the company, even if I was away from work."[38]

Like many of us, Reed put his nose to the grindstone to accomplish a task. However, all that work created burnout, and he realized that he could have been even more productive with his time if he took care of himself.

Have you had similar experiences in your life? You may of accomplished a goal, but at what cost to your health and well-being?

Lady Gaga

Many of us can remember when Lady Gaga broke onto the music scene in 2008 releasing her big hit, "Just Dance" The song took off like wild fire, and she instantly became a household name. Her music video on YouTube has over 273 million views as of 2019. You might also know her from songs such as "Born this Way, Million Reasons, and Bad Romance."

Wanting to do more than just sing commercialized pop music, Lady Gaga decided to branch out into other pursuits.

In 2018 she starred in a movie called "A Star is Born" with Bradley Cooper. The film was an international success grossing over $434.9 million, starting with a budget of $36 million. [39]

Lady Gaga won the Critics' Choice Movie Award for Best Actress and the MTV Movie & TV Award for Best Performance in a Movie.

What is one of her biggest secrets to mega-success?

"*Yoga makes me feel like I can do anything.*"[40]

How might your life changed if you embodied a feeling that you could do anything?

Beyoncé

Another singer that you have definitely heard of, unless you're living under a rock is Beyoncé. Since coming onto the music scene in 2012 with the group Destiny's Child, she has gone on to create a solo music career, toured the world, sang at the Inauguration of President Barack Obama, and inspired millions along the way.

She's a mother, wife, dancer, performer on top of being a singer. Her touring schedule is grueling; her time is limited, yet she stays in incredible peak physical shape. How does someone do so much for so long and not get burnt out?

Besides, eating healthy, and partaking in various forms of physical exercise, she practices yoga. A simple Google search of Beyoncé and Yoga will show you a picture of her doing a one-legged wheel pose."

Beyoncé's worldwide inspiration has even created a type of yoga known as "Namasbey" or "Beyoncé Yoga," which combines Hatha yoga with her music. Classes take place in Houston and Los Angeles if you're looking to try something new.

Adam Levine

Adam Levine became a familiar name in 2002 when his band Maroon 5 had their first hit, "This Love." Levine had been in the music business since 1994 in the band Kara's Flowers, but once the group changed their name, everything took off.

Maroon 5 has produced songs such as, “She will be loved, Memories and Girls Like You.”

Levine lives a busy lifestyle with being an Emmy Award-winning judge on the TV show, "The Voice," a dad, People Magazines sexiest man alive, and touring with his band.

When first touring, he used to hit the gym and lift weights. However, he reported that this left him too bulked up, edgy, and exhausted. He has talked about how he didn't like feeling and that he wasn't centered. Additionally, he had lower back pain, tight hips, and hamstrings as well.

Struggling to find a solution, Levine eventually discovered yoga.

He says the ancient fitness practice has helped him to be "*more focused*" and make better decisions about his life and career. [41]

He has also said,

"I have a hard time sitting still. I can be all over the map," Adam reveals in the new issue of Men's Health. "Yoga has given me the ability to be more focused and make better decisions that come from a clear place. [42]

Imagine what your life could look like if you could make more focused and better decisions from a clear place?

You might not be singing on stage shirtless, covered in tattoos, BUT having that clarity would be life-changing!

Levine's life has been so positively changed and impacted by yoga that when the band is on tour, there is a dedicated private yoga room present. He uses the room to give a focused hour of a customized yogic practice. When performing yoga, he sticks to Ashtanga and Vinyasa yoga. [43] Levine uses that powerful Ujjayi breathe to move his body in many positions before a big show.

Yoga seems to be his cure for the craziness of performing at concerts in front of thousands of fans and touring the world. It's the remedy for having a relaxed and present mind on stage.

Russell Brand

Compared to many of the names you have heard thus far, this individual may be the lesser of the known, but his transformation is quite impressive.

As an actor, he is known for roles in movies such as "Saving Sarah Marshall, Get Him to the Greek, Arthur, and Rock of Ages.

He's also a comedian with stand-up performance shows called, "Better Now, Russell Brand Live, Russell Brand in New York, Messiah Complex and Re: Birth.

Or you might know him as that guy who was briefly married to the talented singer, Katy Perry.

Over the years, he garnered a reputation as a drug addict, describing heroin as being blissful. He was arrested 12 different times on drug charges and even joked he would introduce his drug dealer to singers such as Kylie Minogue.

On top of drugs and legal issues, Russell was also a former self-proclaimed sex addict.

He reported that "Sex is a recreational for me, as well as a way of acquiring status and validation." [44]

Some of us here might relate, have you ever had sex with someone just for validation or to acquire status? Have you found yourself compulsive to that energy where instead of chasing your hopes and dreams, you succumb to basic level drives that lead you astray?

Obviously, sex can be beautiful and is the ultimate merge of divine energy. Still, as Russell points out, it can also be used to fuel basic Ego desires.

Thankfully, Russell found meditation and then yoga.

On September 20th, 2019, he released a YouTube video called, "This is How Yoga Changed My Life,"

Here are some of the quotes from that video [45]:

"I need a physical component of my spiritual practice."

"Moving the body in alignment with the breath, learning to move free from thought constant thought is powerful."

"A sense of oneness and freedom."

"Helps me to live without the kind of physical intensity of different aspects of addiction that I've suffered from. And the same is true of sex addiction."

"For me, it's an important part of overall health."

"A yogic practice is a beautiful all-encompassing system for self-better."

Russell now hosts a Podcast called "Under the Skin," which asks, "What's beneath the surface of the people we admire, of the ideas that define our time and of the history we are told.

He's had guests on such as Tony Robbins, Al Gore, and Jordan Peterson.

If you're looking for more spiritual depth in your podcasts, look no further.

An Invitation To Explore

Now that you are more aware of how some of the most successful people with long-standing careers have used yoga to embrace change,

There is an open invitation for you to explore your ideas and feelings of how yoga would help you to embrace change in your career.

Could you switch jobs and take on a whole new career? Could you spend more time working on what you're most passionate about? How would it feel to have that calm and focus the mind like Adam Levine while you head into your current job?

I'd invite you to explore, meditate, reflect, or journal on what the science of yoga would significantly impact your career.

What would it look like?

Part 3: THE TECHNIQUES

CHAPTER 7

THE LIFE-CHANGING BREATH

"When you own your breath, nobody can steal your peace"

– *Anonymous*

When you were born into this beautiful world, the very first thing you did was take a gasp of air. Someday, hopefully in the far, far distant future, when your time does come to leave this life, you will exhale as you pass away.

Breathing takes place when air is moved in and out of the lungs to facilitate an exchange of gas. You bring in oxygen through your nose or mouth and your body releases carbon monoxide through those same areas.

Your breath also plays a role in speech, laughter, and other expressions of emotions. It even acts as a reflex for coughing, yawning and sneezing.

You probably know the importance of breathing to keep you alive, but how does it pertain to yoga?

Earlier, you learned about how the yoga sutras are a collection of yogic practices written thousands of years ago. Only twice in the sutras are any physical movements listed, and those are about seated postures. The breath, the fourth limb of yoga known as Pranayama has much more information.

Pranayama

Yoga Sutras 2.49 through 2.53 discuss pranayama breath work. Listed below are English interpretations and translations of the Sanskrit writings. [46]

2.49 Pranayama is the regulation of the incoming and outgoing flow of breath with retention. It is to be practiced only after perfection in asana is achieved

2.50 Pranayama has three movements: prolonged and subtle inhalation, exhalation, and retention, all regulated with precision according to duration and place.

2.51 The fourth type of pranayama transcends the external and internal pranayama's and appears effortless and non-deliberate

2.52 Pranayama removes the veil covering the light of knowledge and heralds the dawn of wisdom.

2.53 Then the mind becomes fit for concentration.

After reading Sutra 2.49, you might think to yourself, "Well, I'll never be able to use this technique because I can't perfect an Asana!"

What's important to note here is not the rules and regulations for breath work, but realizing thousands of years ago, Yogi's understood the importance of breathing techniques.

Again, the Sutra's were written more of a guide for living, rather than hard living rules.

Many scholars believe, Patanjali does not fully elucidate the nature of prana, and the theory and practice of pranayama seem to have undergone significant development after him. [47]

Enter Ujjayi Breath, the breathing technique that will change your life!!!

Ujjayi Breath

Pronounced ooh-ja-ee

Ujjayi means to be victorious or victorious breath, some people even refer to it as an oceanic breath. It kind of sounds like Darth Vader from Star Wars when he is breathing in and out through his mask. It yoga, it is used as a breathing regulation technique to enhance your practice. Some have said it is ideal for helping you relax while simultaneously energizing the mind and body.

Krishnamacharya, who taught the founders of Ashtanga Vinyasa Yoga and Iyengar, described the technique as a way to find balance, to be used as a calming breath to increase oxygen, and build internal heat.

A Hawaiian yoga teacher named Wai Lana said, Ujjayi Pranayama "*tones the lungs and encourages the free and healthy flow of prana" while helping to regulate blood pressure and bringing oxygen to all parts of the lungs.*"[48]

The beauty of using this breathing technique is that it gives us control. Throughout our day, much of our body's function is controlled by the Autonomic Nervous System (ANS). The ANS regulates things like your eyes blinking, our natural breath, and our heartbeats. [49]

The ANS is an integral part of our bodies functioning, because it would be absolutely exhausting if we were in control all the time.

However, sometimes, our body can turn against us, such as when we experience anxiety and have a rapid heart rate, sweaty palms, and begin to breathe irrationally.

Ujjayi breath enables us to take voluntary control over our Sympathetic and Parasympathetic Nervous system (PNS). As you learned earlier, turning on the PNS allows our bodies to relax. It helps you transform the internal to you can positively affect how you feel by regulating the length and volume of your inhales and exhales.

BENEFITS

There are countless benefits to using Ujayi breath both in yoga and in many different areas of your life.

Ujjayi uses your cardiovascular system to create a sense of balance throughout your being.

Here are just a few of the benefits: [50]

- Increases the amount of oxygen in the blood
- Builds internal body heat
- Relieves tension
- Encourages free flow of *prana*
- Regulates blood pressure
- Helps yoga practitioner to maintain a rhythm while they practice
- Builds energy
- Detoxifies mind and body
- Increases feelings of presence, self-awareness, and meditative qualities

This breathing technique helps a yoga student maintain a rhythm to their practice, to take in enough oxygen, and to build energy to practice longer. Pattabhi Jois felt that the technique heated the body so much that when sweat came out, the practitioner was ridding themselves of toxins.

The breath plays a pivotal role as a yoga student transitions between various postures, by helping them stay present, self-aware, and grounded in their practice.

Interestingly, you don't even have to link breath with movement to enjoy the benefits of Ujjayi. If you were to sit down or lie down in any posture and use Ujjayi breath for sixty minutes, you would find yourself drenched and sweat with a calm and relaxed mind.

If you're stressed or agitated, you could use Ujjayi breath in any situation. Simply stop what you are doing and begin to breathe. Even just 90 seconds of using this breathing technique will shift you from a flight or fight response to a calm, focused, and energized mind.

How To Perform Ujjayi Breath

In my TEDx talk "Embracing Change Through Yoga," I provided a simple exercise to learn how to use the power of Ujjayi Breath.

Now, we will cover a similar version and expand upon what was presented in the talk.

You can perform this breath right here, right now.

Sitting up straight in your seat:

Take a deep breath in through your nose, fill up your belly, and now exhale out your mouth.

Again, deep breath in through the nose, feel your stomach press against the waistband of your pants, and now out through your nose making an "HAAAA" sound. The noise almost sounds like you are trying to fog up a mirror with your breath.

Now this time, deep breath in through your nose, exhale out your mouth so loud it sounds obnoxious to anyone in a half-mile radius.

With your next breath in through your nose, seal your lips and now breath out of your nose.

Breath in through your nose, slightly constrict the back of your throat, and now breath out through your nasal passages.

You can now continue with this breath, picture yourself imitating Dark Vader from Star Wars.

The length and speed of this breath is controlled by your diaphragm. Aim to keep equal time between breaths and out-breaths.

When you first start making this noise, you might feel weird, awkward, or even uncomfortable. Then when you hear others making the sounds, that feeling might magnify 10x. It's a noise you don't hear too often, and when someone else does it, you might even get annoyed at first by how dramatic they make it sound.

To fully embrace this new noise, you have the invitation to let go of any inhibition. The first time you tried meditating, you may have thought it was strange just to sit down, close your eyes, and just be in silence. However, the more you do it, the less weird it becomes, and you might think, "Why haven't I been doing this my whole life." If you continue to practice Ujjayi, you will also begin to feel the same way.

Ujjayi's Most Important Benefit

Everything you have just learned about Ujjayi can have life-changing benefits for your present and future self. You learned how it can help you on the physical, mental, and emotional levels to increase your quality of life. The best part is that it's free, you don't have to sign up for any courses, attend a seminar, or be part of some online multi-level marketing scheme to reap its benefits.

One of the most powerful benefits is its ability to bring you to the present moment.

Think about it. The present moment is all we have. The past is over, and the future hasn't happened yet. If we can learn to be more in the present, we can experience more joy in our lives.

The beauty of life is finding peace in this exact situation. How often do you think of something amazing that happened in the past such as a vacation you went on, a restaurant you ate at, or even a lover who gave you an experience you'll never forget?

Or how about thinking of the vacation you are going to go on, or the restaurant you can't wait to visit or maybe the connection with a lover that you crave in your Sacral chakra. Your heart rate might even elevate just thinking about that person.

You are human-being. Your mind will wander, is there room for you appreciate all the beauty that is in front of you at this very moment. Can you acknowledge what's in front of you, can you take it all in without judgement?

Even if you have nothing but a chair in front of you. Think of how that chair got there. Someone had to come up with the design, someone had to pay for the machinery to make it, a worker had to be a part of the assembly line, someone had to ship it, a store had to order it, you had to get into your car to get it. Just for a chair to be in front of you, so many things had to happen.

Could you shift your perspective to gratitude and really take it the chair that's right in front of you?

Is there space for you to take in all the different aspects of this chair? The fabric, the style, the color?

When you begin to live in the present, your mind will naturally become calmer, you won't emotionally react to everything in front of you, and you'll find more appreciation for the little things.

My virtual mentor, who I've never met, but has taught me so much from his interviews and Instagram account is a Yogi by the name of Dylan Warner. When you have a chance, be sure to look him up, his poses will absolutely blow you away with what he can do with his body.

Dylan has provided some absolutely beautiful quotes on the present moment that I feel absolutely compelled to share with you:

"Let go of goals. Instead of trying to be better, work on giving your best every day. Better is about the future; your best is now. You can never do better than your best at this moment."...

"When we focus on what we can change in the present and let go of future expectations, we find growth while feeling content with our place on this journey."[51]

These quotes almost feel like a mic drop kind of moment. The more you read it, reflect on it, and even meditate on it, the more depth it takes on. Invitation for you to explore what this means to you.

For me, it was life-changing in that I have achieved many goals in life, but never found myself satisfied. As I'd achieve one goal, I'd immediately be chasing the next goal. When I shifted to just trying to be the best version of myself every day, I found more peace of mind. When I let go of future expectations, I found myself content with whatever came my way.

Now, this isn't to say don't have dreams or aspirations, be sure to take action every day, and work toward something you want to achieve. But is there room for you to allow more space to achieve something even better.

For instance, I am a member of Toastmasters International. For years, I entered their speech contest with the objective of being the "World Champion of Public Speaking." I was expecting to win and was disappointed when I lost. I sat down and meditated on the why behind the reason for wanting to win. I realized that for me, it was about being able to get on stage and share a message, it wasn't even about winning. When I let go of the expectations but still worked on becoming a better speaker, I created room and that opened the door to give a TEDx talk.
Imagine what you might be able to do by becoming more present, still working toward a goal, but letting go of expectations?

If you took a look at Dylan's Instagram page, I'm sure you saw some pretty impressive yoga poses. Some people may look at those pictures and think, "Wow, this guy is showing off."

However, it an interview with the London Real, Dylan talked about these poses.

Known his arm balances and handstands, he discussed how moving into these poses gets him more into the present moment. After much practice, certain poses become easier, and he needs to add progressions to find himself back in the present moment.

In what areas of your life do you find yourself just going through the motions, turning your brain off, and almost becoming zombie-like? Is there somewhere in your life where you can challenge yourself in your day to day to become more present? Could you add a little bit of healthy stress, a little challenge to feel more alive in the moment?

Closing Thoughts

Ujjayi breath is powerful and beneficial for you on so many levels.

With the closing of this chapter, you now know how to use it. As you begin to practice the technique you'll soon see how it can completely change your thoughts emotions and physiology in a matter of no tie.

While this breath is powerful, there is, even more, you can do with this breath. You can take it to a whole other level.

It's great to be present to the moment with a calm mind, but imagine what you could do while using this breath and taking action?

In the next chapter, we will discuss precisely how to do so, how you can take one breath and one movement to embrace change through yoga.

An Invitation To Explore

Now that you are more aware of the benefits of Ujjayi, how it works, and what it can do for your life…

There is an open invitation for you to explore your ideas and feelings of how it felt to practice the Ujjayi breath.

What did it feel like? What did you notice before and after the experience? Did you go for 90 seconds; could you try a whole three minutes?

I'd invite you to explore, meditate, reflect, or journal on how using Ujjayi breath in situations where your stressed, agitated, or just a little unsettled could bring you more peace of mind.

Is there a particular situation or person who drives your mind crazy?

Could you picture yourself interacting with this situation or person from a calm mind?

How might that look?

CHAPTER 8

LINKING BREATH AND MOVEMENT

"Movement is the Song of the body".
– *Vanda Scaravelli*

A common reason many people don't attend yoga or only go to one class and never come back is because they believe the class is too difficult.

Yoga can bring up feelings of inadequacy and negative self-worth. Remember, you read in the beginning that to truly change you have to step into your shadow side and be vulnerable.

Students typically feel something to the effect as, "I am doing it wrong" or "I'm just not flexible, or even "I'm the worst person in the room, this isn't for me."

These negative feelings are shared amongst many new yogis. You might feel intimidated walking into a class and see one person doing a handstand, another individual with their foot behind their head, someone else doing a full split while you might not even be able to touch your toes.

The idea that a pose has to look a certain way is influenced from the styles of yoga that are more alignment based. In these practices, everything is based on the alignment and the unwavering understanding that a pose is supposed to look a specific way. While taking this kind of practice might improve your fundamentals, it can also leave you feeling inadequate and that you aren't "doing it right."

Virabhadrasana A.KA. Warrior 1 is a well-known pose cued in many yoga classes. While popular, it is also commonly recognized as putting many peoples bodies in an uncomfortable position.

Here is just one of the cues from Yoga Journal of how to get into the pose with alignment:

"Turn your left foot in 45 to 60 degrees to the right and your right foot out 90 degrees to the right. Align the right heel with the left heel. Exhale and rotate your torso to the right, squaring the front of your pelvis as much as possible with the front edge of your mat. As the left hip point turns forward, press the head of the left femur back to ground the heel. Lengthen your coccyx toward the floor, and arch your upper torso back slightly." [52]

A problem with this pose is when the back foot is turned 45 to 60 degrees. While the alignment here, is "correct", the back foot turned in that direction can cause many people to experience pain in their ankle, knee, and even hip. When that pain occurs, you think you're doing it wrong or that you're not good at yoga.

Warrior 1 is believed to be derived from Scandinavian gymnastics. Remember, the Yoga Sutra's only mention of poses had to do with seated meditated postures. Many of the yoga poses you see today are derived from Scandinavian gymnastics and modern day Gurus of India who created the shapes.
There is nothing wrong with gymnastics influencing yoga poses.

The problem arises in that everyone's body is shaped differently. A pose such as Warrior 1 might feel easy for one individual, while for another it can cause abject pain. Because alignment based classes focus on getting your body into a shape that might inaccessible for the structure of your bones, people tend to look elsewhere.

There has to be a better way…

It's All About Sensation

Rather than focusing on how you think you look or forcing your body into an uncomfortable shape, there is a solution. There are yoga classes that are grounded in the philosophy SENSATION. A practice that focuses on sensation enables you to feel into your body and shift your attention inward, rather than worrying about how everything transpiring in the external.

For the Warrior 1 pose, if you're in a sensational based class, you have the freedom to play around with how your back foot is placed. You might turn it all sorts of angles, so it feels good in your body. You might even take the back heel off the ground and come into a crescent warrior instead of warrior 1. Tuning into sensation, allows you the freedom and permission to do what's best for your body.

Think about it, you are the expert of your body and everybody is shaped differently. Some people have really wide hips, while others have narrower hips. Men typically have more upper body strength, and women tend to be stronger with their legs. It's okay that bodies are different. Instead of trying to force everyone's body into a particular shape, why not celebrate our differences and enable the yoga pose to enter your body rather than your body trying to enter the pose!

Would you order a meal that you knew would taste disgusting? Would you force yourself to eat something that was too soggy, too dry, overcooked, or raw just because you were trying to force yourself into something? The same thing goes for a yoga pose that just isn't right for your body.

When you give yourself permission to go to yoga for the internal, rather, then the external, everything will change. Your mind will begin to appreciate the mental, emotional, and spiritual aspects of the practice, which will keep you coming back for more.

While the physical component is good for the flexibility and strength of your body. If you're just coming to reap the physical benefits, it's unlikely that you will commit to a yogic lifestyle long-term.

It's Okay to Feel

Whether you're a man, woman, young or old, at some point in your life, a person or situation taught you, it was no okay to feel. That expressing emotions was wrong, out of place, and if you did, you had issues.

When that happened, you began to think it was not okay to fully express yourself, that people would judge you, think less of you, or that you couldn't be in control of yourself.

Evolutionary speaking, women have been known to be the more emotional of the genders. It was seen as natural and judged if a women showed her emotions. However, as society continues to evolve and as women climb the cooperate latter, some things have changed.

Women are now made to feel bad about expressing their emotions. Sometimes it comes at work when they don't want their boss to see them crying. If she does cry, she might be unfairly judged that she cannot handle the job or that she is unstable. It could come from a relationship with a man, where anytime she expressed emotions or cried, her significant other told her to stop, that she was acting crazy or being too emotional.

Sometimes even a mother-daughter connection can leave a woman feeling that she is not able to express emotions.

Country Singer, Miranda Lambert, in her song, "Mama's Broken Heart."

"Go and fix your make- up girl it's, just a break up run an'
Hide your crazy and start actin' like a lady 'cause I
Raised you better, gotta keep it together even when you fall apart,
But this ain't my mama's broken heart"[53]

Clearly, a reference to not be crazy when wanting to express a valid emotion.

Men Too

Throughout history, men have experienced shame from society when expressing their emotions or feelings. Throughout a man's life, at some point, he was told to stop crying by a father, friend, or some other man. Words like, "stop being a pussy" or "what are you a woman?" are typically responses if a man sheds a tear or expresses how he feels.

There is a famous meme of Michael Jordan crying at his Hall of Fame Basketball introduction. One of the greatest NBA players of all time is now known and laughed at for shedding tears, rather than being the greatest basketball player of all time.

Obviously, men don't want to be crying and be overly emotional all the time. There are certainly times where men are allowed to feel upset and shouldn't be ashamed to feel. However, when men are told not to feel and cry, men tell themselves consciously and sub-consciously that crying is something to avoid.

When that happens, men lose the ability to express and feel in many different situations authentically. Men become numb to the world around them and how they feel in our bodies. When a spouse asks what's wrong, they can't articulate how they feel because they don't understand their emotions. If they go to their doctors and they might have a challenging time expressing what is going on inside and where they feel the issue.

While this is truly tragic, the beauty of yoga is that it gives you full permission to feel into your body.

Feeling The Movement

Throughout a yogic practice, there are numerous anatomical, directional and sensational cues. Anatomical cues will move your body into a particular shape (bend, twist, rotate) while a directional cue will change where you are facing (step your left foot back, turn to face the window, etc.)

A sensational cue, however, will allow you to feel into your body. Bend your right leg as you FEEL your right glute engage. Extend your arms up to the sky and become aware of how you are lengthening through your torso. Sit down lower in your chair pose to experience the sensation of your thighs drawing together.

Sensational cueing is an ideal way to enhance the mind-body connection. It takes away the pressure from looking a certain way and instead gives you the freedom to explore how you feel. When you begin to feel more into your body, you become more present. You feel more grounded, calm, centered, and find it easier to focus. You being to LIVE again.

Why You Need To Move

As previously discussed, breath work on its own is a fantastic tool for finding calmness and peace. The only issue is that for many if you're just sitting around and breathing, you aren't engaging in the real world. You might even use your breath work during meditation, but if you aren't using your calm demeanor to go out into the world and do something, you are simply escaping.

The movie "The Secret" is a prime example. There are many interpretations about the message of this film, but the main idea is all about the Law of Attraction. How what you focus on, expands. How, if you ask, believe, and are open to receive your desire from the universe, it will come to fruition.

The Law of Attraction does work; however, it only works for people who are doing one particular thing… Taking Action.

In the word attraction, you find the word action. Action must be taken to work toward what you want and to experience life fully.

You could spend your whole day just breathing or meditating, and you would feel more centered and grounded…

But if that's all you ever did, how would you truly feel?

At some point, you would have the urge to move your body and have a physical experience.

The ancient teachings on breath work are phenomenal, and they are tools we can use to live a more peaceful life.

But consider this... Some of the greatest people who taught this kind of work on breath and how to live a more peaceful life did not have the type of stress, mostly stimulation that we have today.

There are no doubt times were tough, and their teachings still holds true today, especially if you embody them.

However, this about it..

Could you image Buddha sitting in rush hour traffic at 5:30PM on a Monday, driving a small, Ford Fiesta, racing to pick up his kids from daycare as his wife is insensately calling him? Telling him he has to stop at the store and grab milk, bread and food for the dog.

How about the Dali Lama working in a call center, with 10 calls in queue, and a screaming customer on the phone telling him how worthless he is. He's trying to calmly assist the person on the other end, but has to deal with their negativity. Not just one phone call, but these type of calls eight hours a day, five days per week!

What about Gandhi spending Thanksgiving with his in-laws. He's sitting there at the dinner table being grilled by his father in law about why he won't eat the Turkey or drink any of the fine wine? He's trying to have a conversation, but keeps getting interrupted by the NFL game on TV in the other room.

Stress has been around since the beginning of time. However, our bodies for the first time in history are being bombarded with stimulus all day long. If you watch a typical advertisement on television or before a YouTube video starts, you witness many fast-moving jump cuts, loud noises, and bright colors. It's not enough to just drive a car, now you are texting and listening to music and drinking a coffee. Even with the ease of technology, you now feel an internal drive that you have to do even more to get all of your things checked off your to-do list.

When the body experiences this much stimulation and stress, it then holds all of that strain in your body. Your body becomes a prison for trapped emotions, thoughts, and even those feelings that you aren't' allowed to express.
Because you sit down all day, sit in your car and drive just about everywhere, your body can't move and work things out.

Buddha, Gandhi, and the Dali Lama had to walk to get to places. If they wanted to give a talk about their teachings, they walked. They didn't use elevators, escalators, or fancy cars, they had to use their two feet in what was probably encased in no the most ideal footwear.

The only way to get that stress from stimulation out of your body is to move it!

Thankfully, your breath can be your guide.

When you begin to link breath with movement, everything in your life will start to change.

The Power Of Linking Breath To Movement

Can you think of a time where you wanted to do something new, but decided not too? Later you had regret and frustrations that you didn't follow your gut instinct.

Maybe you wanted to speak up in a meeting but kept your mouth shut. You might have wanted to talk to a person you found attractive but were too shy. You thought about speaking with that influential person at a networking event but didn't approach. Heck, you might have turned down a social engagement because you were nervous, intimated, or felt inadequate to go.

Linking breath with movement can completely change how you live your life.

Earlier, we discussed how a yoga mat is your subconscious training ground to re-program your mind. In a yoga class, you're consciously putting yourself in a difficult situation with many challenging poses, balances postures, swift movement, constant changes of directions, and even possibly heat and loud music.

Those moments when you said, "no "are when you decided not to put yourself in a challenging environment. You declined an opportunity and this programmed your brain not to take action. At some point we've all done this. The problem arises as the more you say no, the less chance you'll have to say yes, which would allow you to step into a difficult situation and change your life.

For instance, after I broke up with the love of my life, I thought there was no way I could move on. I spent an hour lying in bed, staring up at the ceiling, unable to move. The thought of moving forward was overwhelming, and I knew it would be difficult.

However, taking everything one breath and one movement at a time enabled me to move forward.

The same thing can happen to you.

Think about something in your life right now that is challenging, something you know you need to do, but still haven't. Or maybe even an opportunity you know would change everything for the better, but you don't' want to take action.

Now imagine yourself confidently stepping into that situation and calmly handling every second of it with ease. You're relaxed, joyful, and connected with the person and situation you're in. You can enjoy the experience because you're in the present moment. There is no worrying about what will happen because your mind is not in the future.

The experience went much smoother than you experienced, and you feel proud and accomplished for handling that moment with such grace.

Much of the stress you experience when it comes to these social situations or actions steps you need to change our life is the uneasy feeling of tension.

Tension

Tension is that space, the silence between words. It's your ability to hold space for yourself and the other person. In fact, it's what connects us.

Many people struggle to find their ideal partner or enjoy the sexual experiences they crave because they can't handle tension.

Most flirting is all about being comfortable with tension. Even outside the bedroom, those award moments with coworkers, your boss, a stranger in public, or the uneasiness of walking into a new environment involves tension.

However, when you begin to link breath with movement, you find a sense of ease in this tension. It' almost like you are performing a moving meditation.

People will then begin to describe you as charismatic, magnetic, they will feel drawn to you.

This beautiful connection is your ability to calmly hold tension and be in the present movement because you were operating with one breath and one movement.

As you continue to read, you will find even more depth on this topic. You will also begin to explore how you can make one breath, one movement a practical and simple to follow embodiment of your life.

An Invitation To Explore

Now that you are beginning to understand the power of linking one breath and one movement

There is an open invitation for you to explore your ideas and feelings of how your life might change.

What situations would you walk into and handle with ease? How would your conversations with others look? How would people's thoughts and feelings toward you change? How would it feel to have that powerful connection with everything around you?

I'd invite you to explore, meditate, reflect, or journal on how embodying one breathe and one movement would change your life, how you take action, and how you see the world.

CHAPTER 9

DISCOVERING THE FLOW STATE

"Those who **flow** as life flows know they need no other force."
-Lao Tzu.

You may have heard of other quotes like, "Just go with the flow" or "Be like water," or even "Just be yourself."

These wise sayings are rich with truth, but what do they really mean? What does it mean to go with the flow? What is flow?

According to our good friends at Wikipedia, being in the flow is,

"The mental state of operation in which a person performing an activity is fully immersed in a feeling of energized focus, full involvement, and enjoyment in the process of the activity. In essence, flow is characterized by the complete absorption in what one does, and a resulting loss in one's sense of space and time." [54]

Or as someone in the yogic community might call it, Being Fully Present. A space where there is no past or future, just yourself lost in the moment.

Heck, even the rapper Eminem said, "*You better lose yourself in the music, the moment You own it, you better never let it go, You only get one shot, do not miss your chance to blow, This opportunity comes once in a lifetime you better lose yourself.*" [55]

At some point, you've experienced some sense of flow. It could have been when you were having a conversation with a friend, playing a sport, having amazing and passionate sex, or even being at a concert. You were so immersed in what you were doing that you lost sense of time while simultaneously being present for the whole experience. You didn't have depression about something from the past or anxiety about the future.

Some yogi's have said these moments of flow are the times when our soul comes alive. Where we drop our Ego and connect with the most profound and most authentic versions of ourselves.

All of us would like to enter more states of flow throughout our day. To experience the moment where we find the beautiful balance of effort and ease.

But how can we get there? What will it take for you to have more experiences like this?

You guessed it... Yoga!

A Class Called Flow

If you google Vinyasa yoga or stop by various yoga studios, you will see on many schedules, a class called FLOW.

The class isn't called, move your body on your mat while you're stuck in your head. It isn't called overthink every posture until you become overwhelmed. And it isn't called look around the room at what everyone else is doing so you feel insecure.

It is called FLOW for a reason. The poses in flow smoothly piece together, allowing you to get lost in the moment. If you've ever spent time in the ocean, in a lake or have surfed at, you can relate to feeling the flow of the current, of being in the water.

As a yoga teacher, I teach what is considered an edgy version of Flow yoga. In my class, there is loud music, constant change of directions, intense heat, and various parts where you are left to flow on your own.

Many students love the feeling of being able to get lost in the music, to move their bodies in ways they never felt possible, and to feel so present.

However, some new students, "HATE" this idea. They have said things like, "this is stupid," "this isn't yoga," or "I have no idea what I'm doing."

Years ago, this would have upset me, but I decided to approach these students with an open heart and really understand why they would not want to get lost in the flow.

Here's an example of a typical conversation.
Yoga Student: "I didn't really like this form of yoga, what was that"?

Me: " That's our flow format, it encourages you to delve deep inside yourself, to use one breath and one movement to get lost in the flow of the class."

Yoga Student: "I get that, but I didn't like it when you stopped talking, and I had to flow on my own, I didn't know what to do."

Me: "Tell me more about that "

Yoga Student: " I felt stupid, I couldn't memorize the sequence, one breath, and one movement was too fast and I felt I was doing it wrong, I was afraid I was going to injure myself."

Me: "It sounds like that brought you to an edge."

Yoga Student: "It did! I didn't like that; I want to be told what to do, I want to hold poses for a long time."

Me: "When a yoga teacher tells you what to do, how do you feel?"

Yoga Student, "I like it because I can follow along at THEIR pace, and it feels good when THEY lead me."

Me: "You enjoy the feeling of being told what to do, to have certainty, and go at someone else's pace."

Yoga Student: "Yes, I do!"

Me: "I respect where you are coming from, it can feel nice to have certainty... but I'm just curious... do you find yourself in class, focusing more on yourself or on the instructor?

Yoga Student: "The Instructor, I really like her."

Me: "When the instructor is not talking, where does your attention lie."

Yoga Student: "I look at myself in the mirror to make sure the pose is correct."

Me: "I feel I understand, you like to go to yoga because you like your instructor, and you want to make sure your poses are perfectly aligned."

Yoga Student: "You've got it!"

Me: "It sounds like you know what you want. This Flow practice you just experienced is all about the sensation, not the destination. It's about turning that gaze within, bringing yourself to your edge, and using your breath and movement to break through that barrier. It's about training your brain that when there is stress, uncertainty, and constant change, you can move forward with confidence and ease. It gets you out of your head, from looking for external validation from others and empowers you to go with the flow of life."

Yoga Student: "Oh... Well why didn't you say that in the first place!?"

What's interesting throughout the conversation is the student's response. From what I've experienced, those individuals who are looking for more out of life, who want to feel empowered and that want to challenge themselves to grow will come back to the practice. Those who live in fear, want to be told what to do, and continuously live in their heads overthinking things tend not to come back.

Now, this isn't to say that everyone needs to go to a Flow class, a person might need something different to get lost in the flow. Maybe being in nature is enough for them. However, from personal experience and connecting with many other individuals, this has been the most powerful tool to live a life in the flow.

Flow On Your Mat

Whether you're in a class that is fully guided or if you do find a format with free flow, you will, at some point, experience the feeling of getting lost in the flow.

One of the best ways to experience this is a continuous yoga practice.

When you first start on your yogic journey, you might experience that you're in your head, overthinking everything. "Was I supposed to breathe here, was that an inhale? Which direction are we going in now" "What did he just say?"

It can feel overwhelming at first as you get adjusted to new phrases, new ways for your body to move, and a new way to exercise. But after some time, you begin to really tune into your breath. As you continue to breathe, hopefully, with that Ujjayi breath, you begin to use your inhales to extend, open up, and with every exhale contract, bring your body close together, bring everything home.

You begin to use your breath to power through movement. You inhale, drop your belly and take your gaze up for cow, you exhale and round through your spine for a cat pose. The breath becomes the driving force for the movement while also linking the two together.

At first, you might flow through a few poses before your thinking brain comes back. You'll realize that little moment was as a massive victory as you were able to be in the moment, to be fully present. Then after a few more classes you might link even more movements with breath finding that more time has passed you by. Heck, you might also go through a whole series of Sun Salutations before your active mind returns.

The feeling is something you have to experience. It is powerful to be able to move your body with confidence without having to think about every single movement.

If you've ever seen a break-dancer in person or on YouTube, you will notice that as they begin to move, they start off at a regular pace. But as each second passes, they move quicker and quicker and quicker before they are moving faster than anything you've ever seen before. When they hit the climax of the movement, energy takes over the crowd because they are lost in the moment. You hear people scream loud, and a feeling takes over your body as you watch.

Now, I'm not saying you will be spinning on your head in a yoga class, but you can experience that feeling of being in the flow.

As long as you continue to practice yoga and link breath with movement, you will have more and more moments of this beautiful state of being.

The beauty of training on you mat is that it will even translate to being in the flow off of your mat.

Flow Off Your Mat

Technically speaking, you do not have to go to a yoga class to live in the flow. There are many things you can do, like being in nature, being in a body of water, or getting lost in whatever hobby you genuinely enjoy. If you've ever shot a firearm, you have no choice but to be fully present.

You can find this feeling of flow without a yoga practice,, but there are two issues that arise.

First is that it's a lot easier to commit to a 60 min yoga class a few times a week than it is spending that much time in nature, in a body of water or working on your hobby, especially in winter times in you are unable to be outside. Yoga can be performed all year round.

Second, is that it requires a lot of will power to continually remind yourself to take everything on breath and one movement at a time. Living in the 21st century already gives you enough to do on a daily basis; to remember to use this technique is not easy, but it is easy to forget.

Earlier, we discussed how yoga is a subconscious training ground to re-program your mind. Instead of exerting effort to remember a technique, you can essentially be like Neo in the matrix and have this behavior downloaded into your brain.

If you use yoga to train your mind, entering the flow state will become something you just do without having to think about it.

Benefits off the Mat

***Better Conversationalist**

One breathe, one movement off that mat enables you to be a better conversationalist.

How so?

Well, instead of thinking of the next thing to say or being distracted by external stimuli, you stay present in the conversation. You begin to listen to understand, not to respond. As you get lost in this flow state, the conversations become more profound and meaningful. You start to connect with the beautiful soul in front of you in a way you never thought possible. The person feels understood, and you feel more connected to humanity. This can improve conversations with your friends, lessen any awkward talk on a date, or making any challenging conversation much easier. Your brain takes on a new way of thinking as people now feel magnetically drawn to you.

How do I know?
Because I have experienced it myself. Before yoga, I was usually thinking of some witty comeback or the right thing to say. The conversation would go nowhere, and the other person would feel frustrated and not listened too.

However, thanks to yoga, an hour could go by before my thinking brain comes back on.

***Better Decision Making**

As we enter the year 2020, we are bombarded every day by so many choices. The convenience of the internet has bought us more things to choose from. Whether it be which app to log-into, which social media platform to check, or the unlimited options and upgrade when it comes to purchase an item.

There is so much information that we can get lost trying to figure out what we truly want. The more we begin to think, the more we get into our heads and fall down a rabbit hole of frantic energy.

However, when you live more in the flow state, you don't sweat these small details. You tend to know what you want and how to get it. In a sense, one breath, one movement helps you find that focus or a sense of knowing which direction to head into.

For instance, when shopping for an item online, you don't get sucked into buying more than you need such as "suggested for you items" on the side of the website.. You had a product in mind, and you tend to buy just that item. You saw a particular t-shirt that you wanted, you find the website and go to checkout. Then the site flashes another product at you, instead of getting suckered into buying it, you almost get annoyed that this item popped up on your screen. It's a similar feeling to when you want to watch a YouTube clip. You want to show a friend an intriguing video. As you pull the clip up on your phone, go to show them, and then a 15-second add which you can't skip comes right up, you feel a sense of frustration because it took you out the flow!!!

It might sound hard to believe, but being more in the flow state has saved me thousands of dollars when shopping online. I'm sure Dave Ramsey would be happy to hear that!

***Be More Present**

Being in the flow state is being in a state of presence. You've been told this concept multiple times already, but it bears repeating as we try to re-program your subconscious mind ;)

From the two previous examples, better conversations come from being present. Only buying what you need comes from being more present. There are countless examples of where being in the flow could significantly improve how you live your life.

What if you're a person who hates your job, you feel the clock takes forever to tick by, and you can't wait to get home?

Obviously, your goal should be to find a job that you love that pays more than you're making now. But as you begin to search for that job, why not start to enjoy what you're doing now by getting lost in the flow. The day will go by quicker and you won't be as miserable. When you do finally get a new when the job you'll have tools to get lost in the flow at your new company.

If this all sounds too good to be true, please do not stop reading this book. I just wrote this whole chapter from 5:30PM to 7:05 PM at Café Nero in Dedham, MA. I only stopped once as a person asked me if the seat next to me was taken.

Additionally, my eyes have been locked on the screen, letting the words flow through me. And trust me, this is coming from a person who continuously lived in their head, over thought everything, was paralyzed to take action, and could never be fully present.

In the next few chapters, you'll learn the practical action steps you can take to embody one breath and one movement.

An Invitation To Explore

Now that you are more aware of the power of the flow state through linking one breath and one movement

There is an open invitation for you to explore your ideas and feelings of how experiencing more states of flow could change your life.

How would your conversations with others look? How would your spending habits change? Could you improve your work performance? How would it feel not to overthink everything? How would it feel to go with the flow of life?

I'd invite you to explore, meditate, reflect, or journal on how living in more states of flow would change your whole existence.

Part 4: The Action Steps

CHAPTER 10

TAKING ACTION TO EMBODY CHANGE

"The art of life lies in a constant readjustment to our surroundings."

- Kakuzo Okakura, The Book of Tea

As you keep moving forward on this journey, you're starting to realize that that change is the only constant in life. You're beginning to understand that nothing stays the same. The person you are today looks much different than who you were ten years ago. You may even noticed changes in your personality, habits, and behaviors. In essence, change has forced you to adapt into a new type of person.

Similar adaptations are observed throughout nature. During the wintertime, birds fly south, bears hibernate and many other animals store food or put on weight for the cold weather. Then when the warm weather returns, the birds come back, bears re-emerge from their slumber, and animals start to actively hunt.

Rather than fight against the elements, every part of nature takes action and embraces change. It's in their genetic makeup, mother nature doesn't have an ego telling them to go against what it instinctually knows what to do. Animals don't attend high school or receive certification training on how to catch their food, they simply know what to do.

Who Else Adapts

Bill Bellichick, one of the greatest NFL football coaches of all time, is known for making successful second-half adjustments in the middle of games. As the leader of the New England Patriots, he watches the first half of a game unfold, making careful notes of what the other team is doing on offense, defense, and special teams. Then in the locker room, instead of being stubborn and sticking with his game plan, he embraces change and makes the adjustments needed to help his team win. After winning 6 Super Bowls since 2001, his record speaks for itself.

Even the sport of Football itself has embraced change. In the United States, there are four main sports, Football, Basketball, Baseball, and Hockey. The National Football League was the first to embrace change with instant replay in 1999. Baseball, however would take another 9 years before adopting the same technology. The NFL was ahead of the curve, knowing that unless their sport changed with the times, they would lose many fans. Today, the viewer ratings for NFL games are much higher compared to Major League Baseball. Numbers vary depending on championship vs regular season games, but feel free to google this comparison for yourself.

Examples are found not only in sports, but in the practice of yoga!

Yoga has learned how to embrace the changing times. As we discussed, if you go to India or follow the Sutras, there are only two movement-based poses, and those are for meditation. Yoga was able to evolve with the times as people wanted to link breath with movement. If yoga did not take on the physical practice, it would most likely be irrelevant in the west. The name Yoga would probably sound even more mystical and strange than it does for many already.

Patanjali wrote the yoga sutras thousands of years ago with 8 specific limbs as a path toward enlightenment.

Today, yoga looks much different with vinyasas, handstands and rap music blasting in class. The adaptation while sounding silly, has created a fun and exciting space inviting more people link breath with movement.

Deep down inside of you, you truly know what you need to do to live your best life. However, through societal conditioning, the media, peer pressure, and not finding time to be quiet to explore your own deepest self, you've lost the ability to embrace change.

Thankfully, getting this ability back is simpler than you might think.

The Action Steps To Embrace Change

What you will now learn is a strong recommendation, and an invitation to explore rather than a requirement of what you have to do.

Before you proceed ask yourself..

Are you ready to finally learn how to embrace change?

If so, here is the solution you've been looking for.

1. Accept Where You Are in This Exact Moment

You may have heard the saying, "leave your troubles at the door." While this saying intends to be positive, authentically, we can say it is TOTAL BULLSHIT.

Think about it, if you go somewhere and leave your troubles or your baggage at the door, what is waiting for you when you walk out?

If this is your mindset, you'll begin to use your yoga practice as an escape from the world. You aren't actively transmuting energy; instead you are re-enforcing a pattern of self-destructive behavior. It's the equivalent of being in a therapy session with a psychologist, you've just had a devastating breakup or loss of a loved one. You're crying hysterically and are struggling to get through the day. The psychologist asks how are you feeling? and you respond, "I'm fine." Instead of being there to dive in deep and work on yourself, you suppress all of your feelings. You put up a wall around the opportunity to heal.

Another way to think of it would be you have severe stomach pain. It's so bad you are vomiting blood and have never felt weaker in your life. Your family is concerned and wants you to call an ambulance. However, you're a person who just wants everyone to be happy and for nobody to worry about. Instead of getting the attention you need, you once again say you're fine.

You might have a tendency to "leave your troubles at the door," because you don't want to bring negativity to a conversation with a loved one, family or friend. Your intentions are pure to keep everything light hearted, but in actuality, you're doing a disservice to everyone including yourself.

People crave authenticity! Authenticity is what connects us, even if it doesn't feel good in the moment.

The key is not to judge yourself when you have negative feelings. You're a human for god sakes, you can't be happy all the time. If you watch the movie, "The Secret" you might even feel guilt for not feeling full of joy 24/7.

Non-judgmental authenticity is what will give you the foundation in beginning to learn about how to embrace change.

As Psychologist Carl Jung said, "Depression is like a woman in black. If she turns up, don't shoo her away. Invite her in, offer her a seat, treat her like a guest, and listen to what she wants to say." [56]

Personally, I feel,

"An Authentic Acceptance of how you feel without judgment is where it all begins. Only then can you turn your darkness into light."

2. Breath with Purpose

Your body is truly amazing as it does so much on its own to keep you alive through the Autonomic Nervous system. You rarely think about your breath because, well, you really don't have too, to stay alive. But ,would you rather just be alive, or would you rather thrive, living a life full of purpose?

Any journey in life starts with the first step.

In your yogic practice, it's your breath. The breath is the life force that drives your practice. It enables you to move forward with confidence and energy. It allows you to move fluidly into the next posture, calm your body down when your heart rate elevates, or even help you get deeper into poses in the yin portion of a class.

Earlier, you learned about the Ujjayi Pranayama breath. What many call, a victorious life force breath. A breath so powerful that just breathing with that technique and nothing else would cause your body to be energized and heat up so much that you would be dripping in sweat from only performing the act for 60 seconds.

If you would like to revisit the Ujjayi breath in-depth, be sure to refer to Chapter 7.

In the meantime, here is a brief reminder of how to perform it.

Sitting up straight in your seat:

Take a deep breath in through your nose, fill up your belly, and now exhale out your mouth.

Again, deep breath in through the nose, feel your stomach press against the waistband of your pants, and now exhale out through your nose, making an "HAAAA" sound. The noise almost sounds like you are trying to fog up a mirror with your breath.

Now this time, deep breath in through your nose, exhale out your mouth so loud it sounds obnoxious to anyone in a half-mile radius.

With your next breath in through your nose, seal your lips and now breath out of your nose.

Breath in through your nose, slightly constrict the back of your throat, and now breath out through your nasal passages.

You can now continue with this breath, picture yourself imitating Dark Vader from Star Wars.

The length and speed of this breath is controlled by your diaphragm. Aim to keep equal time between in-breaths and out-breaths.

Breathing with purpose is your second step in your Embracing Change foundation.

To take this experience to the next level, it's now time to link breath with movement!

3. Linking Breath With Movement

As you practice Ujayii breath, you're starting to understand how just breathing can completely change your physiology.

Now it's never safe to assume anything, but if you are reading this book, I'm willing to bed you are probably not a monk living in the Himalayas or person living off the land in rural, Northern Alaska.

Unlike these individuals, you have modern day responsibilities that you must adhere too. Whether it's working, going to school, raising a family, or taking care of yourself, there are everyday action steps you have to do. Grocery shopping, driving, being there for others, the list can go on and on.

You have so many responsibilities that some days you feel absolutely drained and exhausted. When something challenging or new comes along, a lot of times, you say no simply because you don't have energy. Other times there might be feelings of anxiety that keep you from the new thing you need to do to better your life.

This is where the power of linking breath and movement comes in. Performing and embodying this technique will give you the ability and power to step into all uncomfortable challenges.

Here's how it looks.

You've accepted how you feel.

Even if you're nervous, uncomfortable or angry about something, you're being honest with your emotions. With this acknowledgement you begin to breathe with purpose, giving you a sense of control, creating energy to take action, and enhancing the mind-body connection.

As this is established, you are now ready to move.

But how?

Option 1: Re-Program your Mind--

To engrave this behavior deep into your subconscious, it's ideal to commit to a yoga practice!

In most yogic practice you will perform Sun Salutations, which are designed to be swift and challenging. These sequences force you to link breath with movement. As you begin to perform this behavior on your mat, you will automatically do the same thing off your mat. When a challenging situation arises in your day, you'll breathe and move right into it, taking the whole experience, one breath and one movement at a time.

Now, you might be thinking... "*Yeah great, but I've only been practicing yoga for a few weeks,*" or" *I don't want to take yoga, how will this work for me?*"

Option 2: Will Power--- You can still use the one breath, one movement technique without committing to a yogic practice.

Here a few examples:

You see a person at a social event that you would love to talk to. You feel knowing this person would be a value-added benefit to your life. Maybe you want to be friends with them, networking for business, or even be romantic with this person. You seem them standing in front of you, commanding attention and respect from those around them. You, on the other hand, are awkwardly standing around by yourself with your hands in your pockets.

As you begin to accept how you feel and not judge yourself, you then begin to breathe with purpose. You start to feel a slight physiological change, and start to walk over to this individual. On the way, you begin to breathe and move, breath, and move. (You're not walking like a robot, but natural with your movements.) Along the way, you begin to feel more confident and even talk to a person or two as you move forward. These small interactions build momentum, and by the time you get to the person you want to talk too, you are feeling in a calmer, confident, and more grounded state of mind.

Now imagine if you have just gone up to that person without doing any of this? How awkward would it have gone? What would it have looked like? Have you done something similar to this before?

Another opportunity to apply this technique would be during a job interview. This situation can be uncomfortable for many people because all of the pressure and attention that is centered on you. More likely than not, you need the job, and you feel an added pressure to perform and connect with the people in front of you.

If you are not in a calm, confident, and grounded state of mind, you might feel pessimistic about your chances of landing the position.

Instead of just walking into the room, feeling uncomfortable, you could simply acknowledge how you feel in your car and begin to breathe. Then, as get out of your car link breath with movement as you walk into the building. As you find yourself in the interview, you could breathe and even more your toes up and down to continue the ability to link breath and movement.

You could even use this technique as you sit in the waiting room, as a way to take action instead of getting stuck in your head.

You can even perform this technique if you find yourself single after being in a loving relationship. You know that after breaking up with a person you cared for, it can feel challenging to move forward. The person you thought you were going to spend your life with is no longer your significant other.

After you have given yourself adequate time to go through the grieving process by being authentic, there will come a day when you take a breath. That breath is then linked with movement. Moving forward becomes a little bit easier each day. You start to see =all the action steps you can take to get yourself to move forward with your life.

When you're heartbroken, you feel isolated and disconnected from the world. You see your existence as a dark, and your energy is drained. You don't see a way out or see the light at the end of the tunnel.

One breath and one movement will not get you feeling 100% like yourself over-night. However, it will slowly start to get you back into the flow of life. When you do find yourself around others, you'll begin to feel more connected. As long as you understand it's a process, you will begin to heal and feel better.

As a side note..

If you are currently struggling in your love life, I'd invite you to reflect on this quote from a Madonna song.

In the song, "Secret' she so eloquently says, "*Until I learned to love myself, I was never ever-loving anybody else.*"[57]

Something to think on, or meditate with, if you are trying to attract a new lover.

4. Journal/ Write Down Your Results

"*Time spent in self-reflection is never wasted; it is an intimate date with yourself." -Dr. Paul T.P. Wong.* [58]

Life can pass us by in the blink of an eye. The older we get, the quicker time flies, and before we know it a month, a year or even a decade has passed. Living in the moment and being present is a phenomenal way to live life.

However, every once in a while, it's ideal, stop, reflect, and write down what is happening. When we do this, we can objectively see just how far we have come.

Using one breath and one movement will set forth many positive changes in your life. Every day you will begin to experience little transformations in the course of your day. It could have been things like saying "hi" to a person you never met, raising your hand in a meeting, or embracing necessary adjustments with ease.

As you go about your day, you might your new behavior was nothing special because of how small it was. You might think that you have always performed those kinds of behaviors or taking those sorts of action's

The power of journaling will show you exactly how you've grown and learned to embrace change in your day-to-day. If you kept a journal for a year, you would begin to see that from the beginning of the year till the end, you're almost a completely different and up-leveled individual. The power of putting pen to paper or journaling electronically will show you the factual evidence of the new you.

Typically, in life, we don't realize anything has changed until someone has told us something like, "I love your new hair cut or have you lost weight?" Other times we don't notice it ourselves unless it was something entirely out of the ordinary.

Journaling will give you the power to see it for yourself at the internal level rather than seeking it from external validation. You'll slowly shift your feelings of happiness from the external approval of others to your own inner sense of accomplishment.

By the end of the year, you become a person who has learned to better embrace change and find more joy from within!

An Invitation To Explore

Now that you are more aware of the exact step by step formula to embrace change through yoga,

There is an open invitation for you to explore your ideas and feelings of how these actions steps might change your life?

Is there a specific area that you have not been taking action? Have you not been authentic in that situation?

If you were to take one breath and one movement, how would your life change?

I'd invite you to explore, meditate, reflect, or journal on how your life would look one year from now embodying one breath and one movement.

CHAPTER 11

SURRENDERING TO EMBODY PEACE

"You find peace not by rearranging the circumstances of your life, but by *realizing who you are at the deepest level.*"

– *Eckhart Tolle*

So far, you've discovered the specific action steps you can apply right now to take to embrace change. You've learned about authentic awareness, how to breathe, and how to link that breath with movement. You've acquired more tools for your life's tool belt. You're now better equipped to handle difficult situations that come your way.

You know how to embrace change, but do you know how to embody peace?

Peace Defined

What comes to mind when you think of the word peace?

What are the images that pop into your head? Does peace look like a calm beach or forest setting? Does it look like a Buddhist monk meditating? Or maybe it takes on a whole different image... Do you see an ungrounded hippie spreading a message of peace and love? Or how about protesting getting angry with signs demanding peace?

Peace can take on many different forms.

The best definition I've come across is from Webster's Dictionary. "Freedom from disturbance, or tranquility. [59]

For the purposes of this chapter, we will focus on this definition in order to better achieve peace of mind.

As we delve deeper, realize that embodying peace 24 hours a day, seven days a week, is a lifelong process that many of us will never achieve.

Honestly, though, how could we?

We cannot have light without the darkness, and we cannot have peace without some disturbances from time to time

Think of embodying peace as living more of your day free from disturbances, or finding remaining calm when there are disturbances

There will be times throughout your day with your calmness is disturbed. When this happens, instead of getting upset, give yourself a non-judgment reminder that it's simply a moment to start again.

Steps To Embody Peace

First and foremost you do have to have some sort of daily yogic practice. This does not mean you have to go to a studio, but it mean you have to breath and move with purpose throughout your day. Doing so will enable you to operate with more fluidity, be connected to those around you, and enhance your mind-body connection.

Once that is achieved, you can move onto the two most essential tools you can learn to embody peace:

Meditation and Surrendering.

Tool 1: Meditation

More likely than not, you've come across the word meditation and decided to give it a go.

Maybe you tried it and felt you couldn't do it. Perhaps you did enjoy it, practiced for a while, but life got busy, and you forgot. Possibly, you might be one of those rare individuals who is a life-long meditator.

Regardless of your experience, understanding what meditation is, how to use it, and most importantly, when to use it, it is essential to finding peace on your journey.

What is Meditation?

Many people tend to think meditation is about stopping all of your thoughts. To achieve a state of emptiness and nothingness.

While this might be possible for a few select few, it really isn't the goal of meditation, especially in the 21st century.

Instead of getting rid of all your thoughts, meditation can be used to instead observe your thoughts. Every day, you're always running around, accomplish tasks that are external in nature. You visibly check off items off your to do list, you shop, you meet others, you perform numerous actions which are required to live.

However, if you never go inside, you completely ignore your inner world. Your inner world is the other half of you that is continually calling out for attention. Whether you're too busy, think it's not essential, or are afraid to dive in deep, it's the one area of your life that, when addressed, can change your life in profound ways.

Meditation enables you to become aware of everything that is going on in your head. The biggest mistake meditators make is judging and labeling their thoughts. They think they shouldn't be feeling a certain way or that a thought they have is weird or get frustrated that they can't calm their mind down.

Rather than beating yourself up for whatever thoughts come to mind, simply shift your understanding to the idea that these thoughts are not only normal but encouraged.

Instead of suppressing these thoughts, you begin to become aware of them, and eventually they begin to fade away. The more you acknowledge an idea and the next and the next, the deeper you go. It's almost like finding a station on an old-time radio, you hear nothing but static until you find that sweet spot and everything becomes clear.

The beauty of this process is that you tap into what's really going on in your head. You can see which areas of your life are calling your attention for acknowledgment.

After you perform this technique, you will start to FEEL different.

The best way it can be described is "Taking the Edge off"

If you've ever drank alcohol, you know that after having one or two drinks, you begin to calm down just a little. All that frantic energy that puts you on edge begins to disappear. You begin to feel more moments of calmness, centeredness, and being grounded.

The most challenging part is to accept your thoughts as they come. Not only that, but have the patience to go through the process. It could take seconds minutes or even an hour. Eventually, your brain burns through some much energy that you have no choice but to find a center.

The beauty of yoga before meditation is that it calms your body down so you can explore your mind. For so many people, trying to meditate without physical movement beforehand makes meditation 10x more difficult because they have not only a restless mind but also a restless body.

Yoga, followed by meditation sets you up for success. It's the foundations, that modern-day yogi's use to live a life with more peace.

In the next chapter, there will be a discussion and action step guide to get you to mediate.

For now, let's move on.

To embrace change, you need yoga.

To embody peace you need tool #1 Meditation and tool #2 The ability to Surrender

Tool: 2, Surrendering

The act of Surrender gets a bad rap.

Many think it means to waive ta white flag as an act of being a coward or defeat. That surrendering means to have lost something or that whatever they are fighting for is lost.

From a tactical, military standpoint, surrendering might mean the loss of land, people, economy, or resources.

In your own life, you don't want to give up on all your goals, nor quit everything you're currently doing from a place of being lazy or quitting.

Instead, try to understand the nuisance idea of what surrendering really is.

Surrendering from a spiritual, yogi, path is to get what your heart really wants in life meaning to surrender your: blockages, control, and the idea that you have to do everything.

You still keep the intention of what you want to achieve, but you surrender everything else that can hold you back.

Typically, this involves your ego.

Earlier, I mentioned how I wanted to win the Toastmasters International World Championship of Public Speaking. My ego was determined to win it, I set it as a goal and took action to make it happen. Of course, I didn't even go too far in the competition. Later, after mediating on why I entered the competition, I realized that I only wanted to get on a stage and spread a message, it wasn't about winning. However, my ego wanted to win. When, I did surrender my egoic desires, a door opened for the opportunity to give a TEDx talk.

I let go, created space, and something even more beautiful came through.

Where in your life, might you be able to apply this very same technique?

Are you searching for the ideal partner? Are you trying to find a new job? Are you looking to make a career change?

If you have been trying to achieve something, really explore what it is about that thing or goal? What's the more profound meaning? What's your version of your ego wanting to win a speech competition?

Do you want a relationship because you feel alone or because you feel full and want to share experiences?

Do you want a new job because you're bored or have not found ways to challenge yourself?

Do you find any goal you want to achieve from a place of emptiness to fill an ego need or from the heart to make the world a better place?

This chapter could be turned into a whole book or series of books.

For now, let's rein things in and keep it simple.

You know how to link breath with movement, and you now better understand the importance of not judging your thoughts as they come up in meditation.

Now, you're about to learn exactly how to let go.

It is simple to perform and if do it following yoga and meditation, you'll also realize just how powerful it is.

It's a simple 3 step process you can do any-time, any-place (though, ideally after yoga.) Letting go is an ability you were born with. you don't have to buy anything or rely on others, and this simply involves you.

The three-step process can be broken down into:

1. **Identify the problem**
2. **Allow yourself to experience the problem (FEELINGS)**
3. **Let it up and let it out**

This three step process is heavily influenced by the work of Dr. David R. Hawkins in his book entitled, "Letting Go". [60]

His book goes further into detail about your different levels of consciousness such as grief, angry, depression, apathy and more. If you're interested in delving deeper into those emotions, feel free to check out the work of the late, great author.

For our purposes, the technique you are going to learned has been modified to fit the overall message of this book.

How It Works

The first thing you need to do is *Identify the Problem*. To do this, you must put ourselves in a state of awareness. Find a comfortable place to sit, preferably a chair where you are sitting upright. You could sit down in the lotus position, but for this exercise, I prefer a chair with a straight back.

Place your hands on your thighs with your palms facing up. Close your eyes and begin to become aware of your stomach. Begin to shift your thoughts to any feelings you may have in this area. Become mindful of your gut feelings or what sensations are happening in this area around the Solar Plexus. If something is causing us stress, we usually have some activity going on in this area, try to really FEEL what is going on.

Allow yourself to experience the feelings in sensations without judgment. However, to feel fully present, we need to ground. Keeping your feet flat on the floor, picture roots coming out of your feet, going to the center of the earth. Picture them going deeper and deeper as your root yourself with Mother Nature. Then, take your awareness to the bottom of your spine AKA the Root Chakra. Be with this area and feel your body sinking into the chair.

There, bring your awareness to your stomach. Whatever might be going on in your stomach, it just is what it is. There is no labeling, judgment, criticism, or any thought from the mind. It is merely a feeling that you are becoming aware of and that you are present with. Shift all your energy down to the bottom of your stomach. Allow your mind to empty as every feeling and thought you have come to this area. Even with your breath, you want to bring it all down.

Once you have the feeling, begin the following breathing technique.

- Breath in for 7 seconds, hold for 3 seconds, breathe out for 7 seconds, hold for 3 seconds, and begin again. For those familiar with Pyranic breathing, their technique is 6-3-6-3. Personally, we've found better success with our clients with the extra second for breathing in and breathing out. You will perform 3 cycles

Technique in Action

With your awareness of your stomach:

- Breath in through your mouth for 7 seconds, letting the feelings out of your body.
- Hold for 3 seconds
- Exhale for 7 seconds, letting the feelings out of your body.

With your awareness of your stomach:

- Breath in through your mouth for 7 seconds, letting the feelings out of your body.
- Hold for 3 seconds
- Exhale for 7 seconds, letting the feelings out of your body.

With your awareness on your stomach:

- Breath in through your mouth for 7 seconds, letting the feelings out of your body.
- Hold for 3 seconds
- Exhale for 7 seconds, letting the feelings out of your body.

Continue breathing normally. The next step is to let the feeling come up and come out of you. This is where the magic happens and is an essential step on our journey to healing ourselves

You will perform the same breathing technique; however, this time, we want you to bring the feeling up during the inhale and let it out entirely during the exhale. Picture the feelings rising up your body and coming out of your mouth. The feelings are charged and have broken loose from the previous round of breathing, now let's let them go.

With your awareness on your stomach:

Breath in through your mouth for 7 seconds, letting the feelings out of your body.
Hold for 3 seconds
Exhale for 7 seconds, letting the feelings out of your body.
With your awareness on your stomach:

Breath in through your mouth for 7 seconds, letting the feelings out of your body.
Hold for 3 seconds
Exhale for 7 seconds, letting the feelings out of your body.

With your awareness on your stomach:

Breath in through your mouth for 7 seconds, letting the feelings out of your body.
Hold for 3 seconds
Exhale for 7 seconds, letting the feelings out of your body.

How do you now feel? You should feel lighter, less tense, and more at ease with yourself and the world. If there are still unwanted negative feelings, you may need to repeat the cycle a few more times.

However, if you feel even just a little bit better, congratulations, you have successfully processed these thoughts and emotions. A big difference from what we typically do: escape, wrongfully express, or suppress then. Continue practicing this technique when you feel something is weighing you down or holding you back. You should perform this exercise every day so that your mind is always clear.

Now that you know how to link breath with movement, meditate and also surrender, you have come to discover how to live a life where you can Embrace Change and Embody peace.

In the following chapter, we will discuss a 30-day action guide to get you moving toward the life you want to live. It is simple, straight forward and will give you the exact solution you need.

Before we get there, let's take the time for one more reflection.

An Invitation To Explore

Now that you are learned more about techniques to embody peace...

There is an open invitation for you to explore your ideas and feelings of how living a more peaceful life would look for you.

Is there a specific area that jumps to mind? How would interactions with your family and friends look? How might your job change? How might your own self-talk transform?

How would your challenges look if you felt more at peace before stepping into them?

I'd invite you to explore, meditate, reflect, or journal on how your life would look one year from now from a more peaceful state of mind.

CHAPTER 12

The 30 Day Guide

"By Failure to Plan You Prepare for Failure""
- Benjamin Franklin

Thanks to the internet, any information you are seeking is just a simple click away. All of this information helps to educate us, expose us to something new, and can even bring hope to areas of our lives where when we have previously felt stuck.

The spiritual community has especially embraced this information. Authors like Ester Hicks, David R. Hawkins, Rhonda Byrne, and opened our eyes into modalities of healing and self-discovery. Their ideas are powerful, make us think and open us up too endless possibilities.

For instance, you might, create a vision board, meditate more often, or even go to yoga. Soon, you begin to feel better and enter and up-ward spiral of positive momentum.

However, after a few days, weeks, or months we get busy, life happens, and you forgot to use this powerful tool that created such great inspiration.

Everything was going so well, and then you stopped to doing the very thing that was creating such grand improvement.

What went wrong?

It's simple.

You let inspiration elevate your emotions temporarily; but just like the weather, emotions can be fleeting.

The more you explore this lack of motivation, you realize the problem was that you did not make this new tool, technique, or behavior a HABIT.

As author Octavia Butler said,

""First forget inspiration. Habit is more dependable. Habit will sustain you whether you're inspired or not. Habit will help you finish and polish your stories. Inspiration won't. Habit is persistence in practice."[61]

Some have even said that our life is no more than a sum of our habits.

You might think you have total control over your thoughts and how you behave in your day to day, but in actuality, your habits control over 90% of what you do.

This is something I learned and experienced from practicing yoga. To finally understand the power of habits, has profoundly changed my life.

When I started missing yoga, a few days in a row, I realized life was getting busy and interfering with my practice. I could no longer take a class in the morning because of other commitments.

Rather than get frustrated, I decided to make yoga a habit.

Meaning, every day at 5:30PM, I would go to practice whether I felt like it or not.

This commitment was made because, I realized there will be days where I want to do something and other times when my emotions will sabotage my progress.

When I realized will power can only sustain me so far, I turned to creating habits.

A great book to read on this topic is "The War of Art" by Steven Pressfield. In his book, he highlights and stresses the importance of setting aside time every day dedicated to the project you're working on. For instance, if you have a project that's do for work, you'd set aside the same time every day and use that time to work on that project.

If you struggle to keep a clean home, you will set aside the same time each day to clean. If you need to go to yoga, you will attend the same class time most if not every day to make your new behavior a habit.

As you know, I have been a member of Toastmasters, a public speaking group dedicated to helping adults overcome their fear of public speaking and become better communicators.

Over the years, I've seen hundreds of members come and go. They would start off motivated, enthused, and excited about the club. However, when they missed one meeting, it that turned into two and then three missed meetings in a row. Before long, they might come once every few months before eventually not renewing their membership.

However, the other members who just kept showing up each meeting, committed to making their communication improve, into a habit. While every person's progress was different, after a year of commitment, even the worst speakers became less nervous and more confident in front of an audience.

There’s an expression, that half the battle is just showing up. There's a reason this adage has withstood the test of time. It's because most people simply can’t show up!

If you’re the kind of person who is ready to show up for themselves, the following 30-day action guide is for you.

From personal experience, 30 days seems to be the ideal time to begin to formulate a new habit into your being.

Some will say its 21 days, others 90.

However, there is something magical, about 30. It's typically a whole calendar month, and when you spend a whole month embracing a new habit, your chances to keep doing it for the following months significantly increase.

30 Days to a New You

Days 1-10 Yoga Classes Every Damn Day

The first ten days of your action taking journey will be about getting you out of your head and into your body. The goal is to enhance your mind-body connection, to ground and to center you. It's your foundation to re-connect to yourself.

Even if you're the kind of person who believes that you are a spirit having a human experience, you still need your body to have this earthly experience. It is your soul's vehicle for navigating the earth. It doesn't matter what your body looks like, yoga is about the feeling and function. You're much better off driving a Toyota Camry with a great engine than you are a Ferrari that needs new tires, spark plugs, and a whole new transmission.

The definition of yoga is,

"To yoke, to bind, to bring together,"

For these first 10 days, it's all about bringing your mind and body together through movement.

What does this look like?

Before starting day 1, you will perform a google search and ask everyone you know about yoga studios local to your area.

Know you probably know there are many kinds of yoga studios, and they all have their pros and cons. One is not necessarily better than the other because the goal is to simply link breath and movement.

However, for the sake of this action guide, do you best to find a Vinyasa Yoga of Flow Yoga or Power Yoga closest to you. Some yoga studios have deals for the first month or for new members. You don't have to commit to a year, just get in for 10 days.

If possible, try to go to at least two different studios to experience their instructors to find which one resonates with you.

Most yoga studios, will have a different instructor on Monday at 7PM than Tuesday at the same time. Some yoga studios have instructors that are very down to earth and grounded, while others can be earthy-crunchy. Nothing wrong with either kind, but you want to find one that works for you.

For the sake of the first 10 days, find two studios. One studio can be labeled Studio A, the other Studio B.

Here's what your 10 Day would ideally look like:

Day 1: Attend Yoga at Studio A **(Journal after practice)**

Day 2: Attend Yoga at Studio B **(Journal after practice)**

Day 3: Choose which Yoga studio you like and stick to that one! **(Journal after practice)**

Day 4: Yoga **(Journal after practice)**

Day 5: Yoga **(Journal after practice)**

Day 6: Yoga **(Journal after practice)**

Day 7: Yoga **(Journal after practice)**

Day 8: Yoga**(Journal after practice)**

Day 9: Yoga **(Journal after practice)**

Day 10: Yoga **(Journal after practice)**

What is this journal you might be asking?

After your practice, you will spend 2 minutes writing down how you FEEL. Yoga is a personal experience for so many people, and this is the ideal opportunity and time to explore how you feel. Putting pen to paper to encapsulate your experience. It might seem like just another thing to do, but having post-yoga relaxation and calm mind makes the process effortless. You can even use your note pad or voice recorder.

The goal is to explore your feelings and to connect with your most authentic self deeply. Your true self is the relaxed version of you hidden beneath societal condition, egoic drives, and primal, limbic brain motivations.

On Days 3-10, you will attend the yoga studio the best resonated with you.

*Note- weekend yoga classes usually have different hours than during the week. If you attended yoga at night during the week, you would most likely have to find a morning/early afternoon on the weekends.

Now you might be thinking, attending yoga 10 days in a row is a lot! I don't know if my body can handle it or I'm going be too sore. You might even be afraid of hurting yourself with so much physical activity.

You'd be surprised to hear that when many people come up with these excuses, but still attend yoga, their excuses melt away. They realize they are able to attend yoga every day because they are listening to their bodies when a movement doesn't feel right. Additionally, exercising with just your body weight creates a much quicker recovery time than if you were to lift free weights.

However, if by day 3 or 4, and you do find that your body is really sore, there is an option.

The soreness isn't necessarily negative because you are tuning in to your body and honoring how it feels. The option here is to take a Yin Yoga or Spa Yoga class. These formats are gentle, feature poses that are primarily on the ground and are considered restorative. You can supplement a Vinyasa class if your body needs something a little softer.

After just 10 days of yoga and a little journaling, you'll begin to notice a profound difference in your state of being.

These 10 days are designed for you to not only enhance your mind-body connection but also to learn how to embrace change.

The constant change of direction on your mat, linking breath with movement, and accepting the uncertainty of the next pose will begin to have an impact off your mat.

If you just did yoga for the next 30 days and committed to making it a habit, you'd have a much stronger ability to handle change with confidence.

My whole TEDx talk was centered on one-breath, one movement.

Now, if this is the last door you'd like to walk through on your journey, I humbly thank you. You now have a life-changing tool that will radically change your existence on this planet. I'm honored to have shown you to this entry and that you decided to walk through it.

But, if you're still reading and want even more, there are still two more doorways for you to explore.

Days 11-20: Yoga and Meditation

In Chapter 11, "Surrendering to Embody Peace" not Bankruptcy (ha-ha), you learned how meditation can have multiple definitions. For this part of your journey, it's all about "Taking the Edge off." You'll use meditation as merely a tool to acknowledge your thoughts without judgment. This will enable you to find more of a peace of mind throughout your day. Your meditation for the next 20 days will be all about non-judgment acceptance of your thoughts.

One of the benefits of yoga, is that it calms your mind down to make meditation much easier.

Have you ever sat down to meditate without exercise? It can be challenging, because not only is your mind restless, but so is your body.

Rumor has it that in India, one of the reasons movement came into practice was to be able to help teenage boys get out their excess energy to meditate.

Now you might be thinking, you want me to go to yoga, journal, and now meditate!? How will I find the time for all this?

Luckily for you, there is an efficient method to accomplish all of these feats in days 11-20.

The great thing about most yoga classes is that the last 5 minutes of your practice is reserved for something called Savasana.

Savasana, also known as corpse pose, is a meditative posture where you lie down on your back, typically with your eyes closed and your arms by your sides.

According to the Yoga Journal, "Savasana is a pose of total relaxation, making it one of the most challenging."

The challenge for many is that when thoughts do arise in their minds, they are labled and judged. You however, will be working on not labeling or judging whatever races through your mind.

On days 1-10, you will partake in Savasana, with zero expectations, heck you could even label or judge your thoughts. Try to see what you naturally do for the first ten days.

However, days 11-20 are all about lying in Savasana and observing your thoughts. Most importantly, not labeling or judging whatever arises.

It may sound simple. Days 11-20 take a yoga class and at the end, notice what your mind does. It may seem simple, but simple does not always mean easy.

After the class ends, you will once again journal for 2 minutes, letting every thought, feeling, and emotion come out. You'll be completely authentic with how every second felt. You may have had a relaxing positive experience, or perhaps lying still without judgement was the most challenging thing you've ever done in your life. Be honest with your experience.

Here are days 11-20 in Action

Day 11: Yoga, Non-Judgmental Savasana, 2 minutes of journaling

Day 12: Yoga, Non-Judgmental Savasana, 2 minutes of journaling

Day 13: Yoga, Non-Judgmental Savasana, 2 minutes of Journaling

Day 14: Yoga, Non-Judgmental Savasana, 2 minutes of Journaling

Day 15: Yoga, Non-Judgmental Savasana, 2 minutes of journaling

Day 16: Yoga, Non-Judgmental Savasana, 2 minutes of journaling

Day 17: Yoga, Non-Judgmental Savasana, 2 minutes of journaling

Day 18: Yoga, Non-Judgmental Savasana, 2 minutes of journaling

Day 19: Yoga Non-Judgmental Savasana, 2 minutes of journaling

Day 20: Yoga Non-Judgmental Savasana, 2 minutes of journaling

***Note** If for some strange reason your yoga studio does not have Savasana, there is always an option to stay after class and meditate. If there is a class right after, there is still the option to find another quiet space in the studio or sit in your car or meditate when you get home.

Day 21-30: Yoga, Meditate and Let Go

If you've been active for the last 21 days, there is no doubt you are feeling differently on a mental, emotional, and spiritual level. If you've been journaling, you're tangibly seeing and reading about what is different. Even if you haven't been journaling, you know something feels different about you.

The first 21 days were all about taking action. On days 1-10, you learned to link breath with movement to embrace change. On days 11-20, you learned the beginning stages of embodying peace.

Days 21-30 will dive deeper into learning how to embody peace.

These particular days are all about letting go.

In the last chapter, you learned the letting go technique. You may have practiced it already and felt a little different, or may you struggling with it. Practicing yoga for 21 days in a row will make this technique much easier to do.

Because this technique might take a few minutes, there are options for when to perform it.

In an ideal world, you would attend a yoga class that offers a 5-minute savasana. In the first minute or two, you would simply observe your thoughts and then, for the next three or so minutes, use the technique. Even better, you might know of a studio where you could linger afterward to practice letting go.

If these are not options, find a quiet place to perform this technique. Right, when you get home, in your car, even in a private bathroom if need be.

What you will find is that all of the yoga calms your body and makes your present. The meditation enables you to create a healthy relaxed, and focused mind. The letting go technique allows you to feel more peace.

It's almost like your emptying your cup to fill it with peace. Any negativity is poured out and filled back up with peace and love.

***Note-** Consider this exercise as bathing. You wouldn't want to let a few days go by without a shower or a bath. It's something you want to perform daily.

Now you might be thinking? This is a lot! How am I going to do all of this?! This sounds exhausting!

All valid thoughts, but remember… this our new HABIT!. It will be automatic. It won't be an act of will power and emotional drainage, you will just do it!

Even better news, after 21 days, journaling becomes an option. You have the invitation to stop journaling at this point.

However, because you're creating a new habit, you might automatically do it anyway ;)

<u>Here are days 21-30:</u>

Day 21: Yoga, Non-Judgmental Savasana, Letting Go Exercise (Journaling Option)

Day 22: Yoga, Non-Judgmental Savasana, Letting Go Exercise (Journaling Option)

Day 23: Yoga, Non-Judgmental Savasana, Letting Go Exercise (Journaling Option)

Day 24: Yoga, Non-Judgmental Savasana, Letting Go Exercise (Journaling Option)

Day 25: Yoga, Non-Judgmental Savasana, Letting Go Exercise (Journaling Option)

Day 26: Yoga, Non-Judgmental Savasana, Letting Go Exercise (Journaling Option)

Day 27: Yoga, Non-Judgmental Savasana, Letting Go Exercise (Journaling Option)

Day 28: Yoga, Non-Judgmental Savasana, Letting Go Exercise (Journaling Option)

Day 29: Yoga Non-Judgmental Savasana, Letting Go Exercise (Journaling Option)

Day 30: Yoga Non-Judgmental Savasana, Letting Go Exercise (Journaling Option)

Habit Achieved!

And there you have it. A written formula for success. It's a simple, straight forward solution to learning how to Embrace Change and Embody Peace.

If you start this journey and miss a day, don't beat yourself up. Just keep moving forward. In an ideal world, you will complete every part of the 30 days for 30 days, but life does happen.

Simply use the distraction or missed opportunity as a chance to start again.

After 30 days of yoga has been achieved, you can begin to take a day or two off from a yoga class. On your "off" yoga studio days, you'll still be performing yoga as you'll find yourself navigating the world with one breath and one movement ;)

An Invitation To Explore

Now that you are learned about the 30-day action guide...

We wanted to extend an open invitation for you to explore your ideas and feelings of how reading this 30 day commitment made you feel?

Is there any resistance that arises from what your read? Do you feel that resistance in any part of your body? If you're excited for the opportunity explore more about how that makes you feel?

Open invitation for you to explore, meditate, reflect, or journal on how your life would look if you were to complete all 30 days of the action guide and beyond

FINAL THOUGHTS

It has been an honor to be your guide and share with you the wisdom of how Yoga, Meditation, and Surrendering can enable you to embrace change and embody peace.

One breath and one movement is the foundation of your new way of being.

It will guide you through difficult times, ground you, give you peace of mind and enable you to confidently handle situations that come your way.

It will allow you to say goodbye to that old version of you that did not raise their hand when they should have, approached someone unfamiliar for a conversation or didn't shine their light when it was needed.

It will set forth in motion a new path for you to walk. One that is led with love, trust, and a knowingness that you are the creator of your life. That you have the power to get what you want and to embrace all uncertainty.

If you choose to build upon your foundation with embodying peace, you now have even more powerful tools to live a life of harmony both in your internal and external worlds.

My fellow yogi, you've always had the answer to living your ideal life. You've been searching for answers outside of you when the solution was hidden right beneath your nose this entire time.

Now all you have to do to elevate yourself, to shine brighter, and to live the life of your dreams is to start with ONE BREATH and ONE MOVEMENT.

Namaste,

Dan Edelston

Yoga Teacher (RYT)
TEDx Speaker

Want Even More?

Follow me on Instagram: Dan.Edelston

Or Checkout www.OneBreathOneMovement.com

Here you'll find follow along videos to enhance your yogic practice.

Additionally, you'll learn more upcoming yoga retreats worldwide!

NAMASTE

Works Cited

Marrs, P. (2017, February 10). If You're Not Growing You're Dying. Retrieved December 13, 2019, from http://www.piercemarrs.com/2016/08/if-youre-not-growing-youre-dying/

[2] Singer, J. (2018, October 8). The Only Constant Is Change. Retrieved December 13, 2019, from https://psychcentral.com/lib/the-only-constant-is-change/

[3] Metathesiophobia (Fear of Change). (2019). Retrieved from https://psychtimes.com/metathesiophobia-fear-of-change/

[4] Marks, H. (2011, April 29). Stress Symptoms. Retrieved December 13, 2019, from https://www.webmd.com/balance/stress-management/stress-symptoms-effects_of-stress-on-the-body

[5] Wei, M. (2015). 5 Ways Stress Hurts Your Body, and What to Do About It. Retrieved December 13, 2019, from https://www.psychologytoday.com/us/blog/urban-survival/201505/5-ways-stress-hurts-your-body-and-what-do-about-it

---

[6] Fischer, M. J., Riedlinger, K., Gutenbrunner, C., & Bernateck, M. (2009). Influence of the Temporomandibular Joint on Range of Motion of the Hip Joint in Patients With Complex Regional Pain Syndrome. *Journal of Manipulative and Physiological Therapeutics*, *32*(5), 364–371. https://doi.org/10.1016/j.jmpt.2009.04.003

[7] Gudmestad, J. (2011). How to Stretch and Strengthen the Psoas. Retrieved from https://yogainternational.com/article/view/how-to-stretch-and-strengthen-the-psoas

[8] Zetlin, M. (2019, November 1). Blockbuster Could Have Bought Netflix for $50 Million, but the CEO Thought It Was a Joke. Retrieved December 13, 2019, from https://www.inc.com/minda-zetlin/netflix-blockbuster-meeting-marc-randolph-reed-hastings-john-antioco.html

[9] Yarow, J. (2011, September 16). All The Dumb Things RIM's CEOs Said While Apple And Android Ate Their Lunch. Retrieved December 13, 2019, from https://www.businessinsider.com/rim-ceo-quotes-2011-9?international=true&r=US&IR=T

[10] BlackBerry Net Worth 2006-2019 | BB. (2019). Retrieved December 13, 2019, from https://www.macrotrends.net/stocks/charts/BB/blackberry/net-worth

[11] Martin, E. (2017, September 12). Investment fail: Why Apple's little-known third co-founder sold his 10% stake for $800. Retrieved December 13, 2019, from https://www.cnbc.com/2017/09/12/apples-third-co-founder-ronald-wayne-sold-his-stake-for-800.html

[12] Ronald Wayne Net Worth. (2019, November 12). Retrieved December 13, 2019, from https://www.celebritynetworth.com/richest-businessmen/ronald-wayne-net-worth/

---

[13] Sippell, M. (2018, September 7). Danny Aiello, "Do the Right Thing" and "Moonstruck" Actor, Dies at 86. Retrieved December 13, 2019, from https://variety.com/2018/film/news/burt-reynolds-turned-down-roles-bond-solo-1202930436/

[14] Guerrasio, J. (2018). Burt Reynolds was such a screen icon that even the list of roles he turned down is legendary, from James Bond to Han Solo. Retrieved December 13, 2019, from https://www.businessinsider.com/iconic-roles-burt-reynolds-turned-down-2018-9

[15] Clairmont, N. (2018, October 6). "Those Who Do Not Learn History Are Doomed To Repeat It." Really? Retrieved December 13, 2019, from https://bigthink.com/the-proverbial-skeptic/those-who-do-not-learn-history-doomed-to-repeat-it-really

[16] Showalter, D. (2019). William Howe | British military commander. Retrieved December 13, 2019, from https://www.britannica.com/biography/William-Howe-5th-Viscount-Howe

[17] Wikipedia contributors. (2019, December 6). Yoga Sutras of Patanjali. Retrieved December 13, 2019, from https://en.wikipedia.org/wiki/Yoga_Sutras_of_Patanjali

[18] Wikipedia contributors. (2019, December 6). Yoga Sutras of Patanjali. Retrieved December 13, 2019, from https://en.wikipedia.org/wiki/Yoga_Sutras_of_Patanjali

[19] Palmer, B. E. (2014, April 23). sutra 2.30: outward connections. Retrieved December 13, 2019, from http://www.yoga216.com/sutra-2-30-outward-connections/

[20] MacGregor, K. (2018, November 26). Yogi Assignment: 5 Ways to Put the Niyamas Into Practice Right Now. Retrieved December 13, 2019, from https://www.yogajournal.com/yoga-101/ways-to-put-the-niyamas-into-practice-right-now

---

[21] Burgin, T. (2019, October 17). Tantra Yoga – Defined and Demystified •. Retrieved December 13, 2019, from https://www.yogabasics.com/learn/tantra-yoga-demystified/

[22] Yuvan, J. (2013). Swami Vivekananda and Chicago's Role in Bringing Yoga to America. Retrieved December 13, 2019, from http://yogachicago.com/2013/12/swami-vivekananda-and-chicagos-role-in-bringing-yoga-to-america/

[23] Rub the sweat during the practice. (2019, November 16). Retrieved December 13, 2019, from https://taysp.com/rub-the-sweat-during-the-practice/

[24] What Is Cortisol? (2017, February 6). Retrieved December 13, 2019, from https://www.webmd.com/a-to-z-guides/what-is-cortisol

[25] Woodyard, C. (2011). Exploring the therapeutic effects of yoga and its ability to increase quality of life. *International Journal of Yoga*, *4*(2), 49. https://doi.org/10.4103/0973-6131.85485

[26] Choi, M. D. (2017). The Effects of Vinyasa Yoga on Cardiovascular and Physical Fitness as well as Psychological Profiles of Well-being. *Faseb*, *31*(1).

[27] Woodyard, C. (2011b). Exploring the therapeutic effects of yoga and its ability to increase quality of life. *International Journal of Yoga*, *4*(2), 49. https://doi.org/10.4103/0973-6131.85485

[28] Woodyard, C. (2011b). Exploring the therapeutic effects of yoga and its ability to increase quality of life. *International Journal of Yoga*, *4*(2), 49. https://doi.org/10.4103/0973-6131.85485

[29] Breit, S., Kupferberg, A., Rogler, G., & Hasler, G. (2018). Vagus Nerve as Modulator of the Brain–Gut Axis in Psychiatric and Inflammatory Disorders. *Frontiers in Psychiatry*, *9*. https://doi.org/10.3389/fpsyt.2018.00044

---

[30] Boston University Medical Center. (2012, March 6). Yoga helps ease stress related medical and psychological conditions, study suggests. *ScienceDaily*. Retrieved December 10, 2019 from www.sciencedaily.com/releases/2012/03/120306131644.htm

[31] Polsgrove, Mj., Eggleston, B., & Lockyer, R. (2016). Impact of 10-weeks of yoga practice on flexibility and balance of college athletes. *International Journal of Yoga*, *9*(1), 27. https://doi.org/10.4103/0973-6131.171710

[32] Nóra Kerekes et al. Imprisoning Yoga: Yoga Practice May Increase the Character Maturity of Male Prison Inmates, *Frontiers in Psychiatry* (2019). DOI: 10.3389/fpsyt.2019.00406

[33] Wachob, J. (2012). Robert Downey Jr Gets His Yoga On! | Awaken. Retrieved December 13, 2019, from https://www.awaken.com/2012/06/robert-downey-jr-gets-his-yoga-on/

[34] Celebrities. They're Just Like Us. (2017, February 13). Retrieved December 13, 2019, from https://barefeetpoweryoga.com/community-news/celebrities-theyre-just-like-us/

[35] Week 32 - a metaphor for life. (2017, February 6). Retrieved December 13, 2019, from https://www.yogamatters.com/blog/week-32-metaphor-life/

[36] Lambert, J. (2017, January 15). The Tao Of Tom: How Tom Brady Uses An 80-20 Diet, Meditation, Yoga & One Book To Age Backwards. Retrieved 2019, from https://www.feelguide.com/2017/01/15/the-tao-of-tom-how-tom-brady-uses-an-80-20-diet-meditation-yoga-one-book-to-age-backwards/

[37] Mullaney, T. (2017, March 10). How Reed Hastings grew Netflix from zero to $60 billion in 20 years. Retrieved December 13, 2019,

from https://www.cnbc.com/2017/03/10/lessons-from-netflix-founder-reed-hastings-20-year-60-billion-run.html

[38] Yeh, C. (2018, June 9). CS183C Session 16: Reed Hastings. Retrieved December 13, 2019, from https://medium.com/cs183c-blitzscaling-class-collection/cs183c-session-16-reed-hastings-4e1058d2439f

[39] Wikipedia contributors. (2019b, December 13). A Star Is Born (2018 film). Retrieved December 13, 2019, from https://en.wikipedia.org/wiki/A_Star_Is_Born_(2018_film)

[40] Journal, E. (2011, February 27). "Yoga makes me feel like I can do anything. Retrieved December 13, 2019, from https://www.elephantjournal.com/2011/02/yoga-makes-me-feel-like-i-can-do-anything

[41] Men's Health. (2014, December 20). Strength, focus and balance: Adam Levine's intense yoga workout. Retrieved December 13, 2019, from https://www.foxnews.com/health/strength-focus-and-balance-adam-levines-intense-yoga-workout

[42] Adam Levine On Yoga Making Him More Successful: "I Don't Know What I'd Do Without It." (2013, January 30). Retrieved December 13, 2019, from https://www.capitalfm.com/artists/maroon-5/news/adam-levine-yoga-love/

[43] McFarland, M. (2019). Adam Levine Yoga Workout. Retrieved December 13, 2019, from https://yoga.lovetoknow.com/about-yoga/adam-levine-yoga-workout

[44] "I was in an orgy ... but it felt like it was being directed by Mike Leigh." (2018b, February 22). Retrieved December 13, 2019, from https://www.theguardian.com/books/2007/nov/12/biography.mikeleigh

[45] Brand, R. (2019). YouTube [YouTube]. Retrieved December 13, 2019, from https://www.youtube.com/watch?v=D31AtqxxJb0

[46] Yoga Sutras 2.49 to 2.53 – Pranayama | KEYoga. (2018). Retrieved December 14, 2019, from https://www.karineisen.com/yoga-sutras-2-49-to-2-53-pranayama/

[47] G. C. Pande, Foundations of Indian Culture: Spiritual Vision and Symbolic Forms in Ancient India. Second edition published by Motilal Banarsidass Publ., 1990, p. 97.

[48] Wikipedia contributors. (2019a, August 4). Ujjayi breath. Retrieved December 14, 2019, from https://en.wikipedia.org/wiki/Ujjayi_breath

[49] DerSarkissian , C. (2017). How can diseases of the autonomic nervous system cause fainting? Retrieved December 14, 2019, from https://www.webmd.com/brain/qa/how-can-diseases-of-the-autonomic-nervous-system-cause-fainting

[50] Eisler, M. (2016). Learn the Ujjayi Breath, an Ancient Yogic Breathing Technique. Retrieved December 14, 2019, from https://chopra.com/articles/learn-the-ujjayi-breath-an-ancient-yogic-breathing-technique

[51] Dylan Werner's Up for a Challenge – aloyoga blog. (2018). Retrieved December 14, 2019, from http://blog.aloyoga.com/2018/11/dylan-werners-up-for-a-challenge/

[52] YJ Editors. (2017, May 15). Warrior I Pose. Retrieved December 14, 2019, from https://www.yogajournal.com/poses/warrior-i-pose

[53] **Mama's Broken Heart Lyrics.** (n.d.). *Lyrics.com.* Retrieved December 14, 2019, from https://www.lyrics.com/lyric/24478416/Miranda+Lambert.

---

[54] Wikipedia contributors. (2019b, November 17). Flow (psychology). Retrieved December 14, 2019, from https://en.wikipedia.org/wiki/Flow_(psychology)

[55] **Lose Yourself Lyrics.** (n.d.). *Lyrics.com.* Retrieved December 14, 2019, from https://www.lyrics.com/lyric/6882471/Eminem.

[56] A quote by C.G. Jung. (n.d.). Retrieved December 14, 2019, from https://www.goodreads.com/quotes/9252695-depression-is-like-a-woman-in-black-if-she-turns

[57] **Secret Lyrics.** (n.d.). *Lyrics.com.* Retrieved December 14, 2019, from https://www.lyrics.com/lyric/2737743.

[58] Self-Reflection. (2014, September 22). Retrieved December 14, 2019, from https://paultpwong.wordpress.com/2014/09/22/self-reflection-2/

[59] Definition of PEACE. (2019). Retrieved December 14, 2019, from https://www.merriam-webster.com/dictionary/peace

[60] Hawkins, D. R. (2014). *Letting Go: The Pathway of Surrender*. Carlsbad,CA: Hay House, Incorporated.

[61] A quote from Bloodchild and Other Stories. (n.d.). Retrieved December 14, 2019, from https://www.goodreads.com/quotes/181907-first-forget-inspiration-habit-is-more-dependable-habit-will-sustain

FEEL FREE TO USE THESE BLANK PAGES TO TAKE NOTES

www.ingramcontent.com/pod-product-compliance
Lightning Source LLC
Chambersburg PA
CBHW030103070426
42448CB00037B/913

* 9 7 8 0 9 9 8 2 8 8 3 9 0 *